Contrary to today's populist rage against the very idea of government, John Luthy reminds us that public servants do serve the public, after all. His prescriptions for how such leaders can and should actually lead are as urgent now as they are overdue. As he says, the mounting challenges we face as a society care not a whit about the next election cycle. So John's strategy for finally dealing with difficult issues that can no longer be avoided is itself a public service.

> — *Rob McManamy*
> *former Editor*
> *Public Works magazine*
> *Chicago, Illinois*

As we struggle with shrinking budgets and rising public expectations, we need to look for new ways to deliver exceptional public programs and services. John Luthy has opened our eyes to the possibility that solutions to these challenges are within our reach through strategic planning. John has made the complex seem simple and the hidden seem obvious with his "Tai-Chi" approach to a planning process that builds teams, ownership, and, most importantly, identifies solutions. His affable style, experience in the public sector, quick wit, and humor makes this an entertaining, informative, and applicable read on strategic thinking and planning.

> — *Kent Cash, Director*
> *Department of Public Works*
> *Cowlitz County, Washington*

John Luthy is a great thinker. We have been very fortunate to have him on the faculty of the *Northwest Community Development Institute*. Each year, his classes are extremely well-received by community and economic development professionals who always want more time with him.

Through his humor, real-life stories and keen perspective, he provides realistic strategies and solutions to complex issues and uncertain futures communities and organizations face on a daily basis. His focused and passionate presentations show those who listen how to take the quantum leap from inaction to a desired future.

— *Gloria Mabbutt, Director*
Northwest Community Development
Institute
Boise, Idaho

I was involved with various aspects of strategic and comprehensive planning for the State of Arizona Department of Parks and Recreation for much of my professional career. Some years ago, I had the considerable fortune of working with Dr. John Luthy to develop a strategic plan for an organization in Western Arizona. John's simple, yet innovative planning approach and expertise in public management, along with my approach to creative grant sourcing, converged perfectly, allowing us to craft an exceptional plan. This book has it all ... a simple, applicable approach to planning that will open new horizons for public managers in every discipline. Whether you are a department director, elected official or program manager, put this book on your 'must read' list.

— *Don Myers, President,*
Rural Consultant Services
Former Resource Planning Manager
Arizona Department of Parks and Recreation

John Luthy has a rare skill; he is able to make strategic planning clear, understandable, and enjoyable at the same time. But he not only presents a surprisingly clear METHOD of strategic planning, he is available to assist in the step-by-step PROCESS which he advocates, then guide organizations to produce workable, measurable action plans. John communicates effectively and effortlessly to his listeners; he has tried, tested and perfected his methods and can justifiably be called an expert in strategic thinking and planning.

I first heard John teach at the Northwest Community Development Institute and had the pleasure of introducing him to the Nevada Commission on Economic Development. In late 2008, John collaborated with us to develop a strategy for economic diversification for the State of Nevada. The finished product helped confirm the role and legitimacy of the agency during the 2009 State Legislative Session.

> — *J. Des Craig*
> *Director, Rural Community Development*
> *Nevada Commission on Economic*
> *Development*
> *Carson City, Nevada*

John challenges us to not only work "in" the organization, but also "on" the organization. His outline for strategic planning is an excellent tool for those who accept the challenge. He advises that, "You call the meeting!" when a need arises to convene individuals to remedy an issue. After several years, his planning work continues to benefit our organization.

> — *Steve Masters, P.E.*
> *Lincoln Public Works and Utilities*
> *Lincoln, Nebraska*

PLANNING
THE
FUTURE

A Guide to Strategic Thinking and Planning for
Elected Officials, Public Administrators and
Community Leaders

JOHN F. LUTHY

Planning the FUTURE
A guide to strategic Thinking and Planning for Elected Officials, Public Administrators and Community Leaders.

Borderline Publishing
406 S. 3rd St.
Boise, ID 83702
www.borderlinepublishing.com

ISBN 978-1936408078 (Paperback)

Cover design by Tara Mayberry

Printed in the United States of America on post-consumer recycled paper

*This book is dedicated to the talented men and
women who serve in federal, state and local
government. You are at the helm during a difficult
time of change, challenge and transformation. As
you chart a path toward an uncertain future,
please know that you are admired and appreciated.*

Table of Contents

Foreword

When John Luthy asked if I was interested in writing the Foreword for this book, I jumped at the opportunity. But then, I've always been the kind of guy who is eager to take on new challenges. That's what I did when Mayor Chris Beutler asked me to be the Director of Public Works and Utilities for Lincoln, Nebraska. I knew well the enormous challenge and responsibility of that job. Little did I know that I would have the privilege of working with John Luthy in developing the department's first published strategic plan, then completing an entire Executive Planning System that has become a national model. It seems natural and fitting that I share some of that experience and how I became a 'futurist.'

It turns out that I have always been a 'futurist.' Many of you are as well, although you may not yet realize it. Whether you are an elected or appointed official, or a career public service professional, when you read this book you'll find yourself nodding in agreement… and occasionally chuckling about the observations and insights John offers and uses to illustrate his straightforward, no-nonsense approach to public agency planning.

So, what brought me to this point? What makes me want to be, and need to be, a 'futurist?' As a professional engineer with 23 years in private practice, I have had the privilege of working for dozens of communities (large and small) as an external consultant. During that time, my wife and I created two successful independent businesses that are heavily oriented to customer service. I grew up in a successful family business and while at the University of Nebraska, started coaching at the high school level and have continued coaching youth sports for the past 28 years. I've slowed down a little, but until a few years ago I still competed as an athlete. When viewed as a composite, you might recognize that I approach every aspect of personal and professional life with an entrepreneurial and competitive spirit. I'm passionate about my profession; I'm passionate about sports and competition; and I have now made the connection between the aspects of providing public services and channeling the elusive human performance elements required to make it all happen. Through this journey, I have discovered that technical knowledge, administrative skills, political acumen, and a team approach all converge through a properly executed strategic planning process. My focus is on the future and, along with my fellow public managers, I have a desire to help make this an exceptional public organization. I want Public Works and Utilities to be in a position to repeat what it does well, to continuously improve, and to consistently showcase its contributions to the community. Similar to most public officials and administrators, I want to be proud of the legacy I leave for this community.

For me, perhaps the single most important point that John makes is to expose the myth that government (or public agencies) should be run like private business. Like many of you, I've heard private sector business leaders redundantly express that "...we should manage government like a business." It has been the battle cry of countless politicians on the campaign trail...a promise to 'fix' government, even with the best intentions, relentlessly pounding old-style business planning into a unique public service environment has never quite fulfilled its promise. Certainly, public administrators should be professional and serve in a business-like fashion, but at the same time recognize that government is not private enterprise. Using public works as an example, the public service aspect of meeting the 24/7/365 demands of providing safe drinking water, clean wastewater, effective and safe public transportation, solid waste management, storm water management, emergency operations, safe streets etc. trumps the profit motive that drives private business planning. One philosophy isn't better than the other; they're just different and simply must be approached differently. John clearly defines the philosophical variances then methodically describes public planning process mechanics systematically and effectively.

When I was asked to serve as the Director of Public Works and Utilities in 2008, I assumed responsibility for the largest department in the City of Lincoln. The department has over 550 employees and the average tenure is in the vicinity of 30 years of service. While small compared to some mega cities, our annual operating budget is approximately $100 million, with annual CIP ranging from $60 to $90 million. So I was pleased (and a little relieved) to find that strategic planning was underway. My predecessor had already engaged John Luthy to conduct training and assist with early stage planning. John's coaching had moved the department to the point where managers were ready to create the first fully integrated strategic plan that linked directly to the city's performance budget. As a team, we undertook the challenge with deep commitment. The process of strategic thinking was not always easy, but nothing worthwhile ever is. However, the process was clear, concise and fully connected to reality. Identifying creative ideas, goals, issues, actions, outcomes, etc. was not particularly difficult. The staff was already keenly aware of issues and desired outcomes. They were already prepared to present great ideas and were full of strategies and action plans. The only thing lacking was a single, straightforward, easily understood and sustainable planning approach. The department had many voices but needed a single language. John introduced that language and helped integrate it into a plan that fits the needs and realities of local government. For public works, the process has been very powerful, but the system would be equally potent for education, law enforcement, fire, public health, human services, libraries, clerks, treasurers, coroners, planning and zoning, building departments, homeland security, airports, and any other public agency. Its beauty lies in its simplicity and direct application to government.

Lincoln's Public Works and Utilities Department did not create a perfect plan overnight. It took a few years. During that time, John visited Lincoln to mentor, coach and encourage. He reviewed the work of the many authors who had diligently written plans that fit the *Prepared for Challenge* formula. To generate support and build a planning culture, we involved staff at all levels, including division heads, section managers, supervisors, crew leaders, production staff and administrative support. During a recent meeting with staff at Lincoln Water System's production facility, I used the new Strategic Plan as a prop to remind staff at all levels of our commitment to quality and public service. I held it up and asked for a show of hands to see if everyone was aware that we had a plan. All hands were raised. I then asked who had actually worked on part of the plan. Of those present, at least 30 out of 35 raised their hands, from the managers to the maintenance crews.

I continue to be amazed by the level of understanding and recognition of key issues and the courage to acknowledge future challenges. LWS management, like all of our divisions, had engaged everyone in the process. They know the plan exists, why it is there and how to use it. More critically, they created the planning metrics and understand they are accountable for measured performance. The message is clear: a properly conducted planning process that engages staff at all levels develops an employee culture that understands planning and knows every aspect of plan content. Very simply, they wrote it and know how to use it.

I'm proud to report that within three years, not only did we produce a highly detailed and measurable strategic plan, we were then able to create a meaningful Annual Report. In the second year, we produced a Strategic Plan, an Operations Plan, an Internal Improvement Plan, and an Annual Report. Year Three again produced each executive planning element with various refinements. It's now a complete Executive Planning Suite. For each division and section, I am now able to track progress against strategic goals, objectives, strategies and actions. Everything rolls up and we move forward to the next year with meaningful updates. My staff has created templates that make it easy to monitor and track progress as we go. Each element of the executive planning process is solid and improves each year. Achieved objectives are 'checked-off' and issues or concerns are noted directly in the Strategic Plan as the department moves through the year. At the end of the year, all progress and notations are added to the plan and it is recast into the Annual Report. In that way, all original plan language remains intact along with actual progress status and notations. The Annual Report serves as a platform for the next Strategic Plan. John has been with us every step of the way, offering support, advice, and encouragement. His coaching kept us on track and on task.

The process requires commitment and discipline; along with dedicated staff and adequate time. Once the language, process and format are learned, it is remarkable how fast a plan can be developed and easily sustained year to year. When is planning done? Well…never. Even when all elements are in place, you must realize that it remains a work in progress. But each year, the effort to create the next annual plan gets easier and less time-consuming. When the Mayor asks questions of the Department Directors, I merely have to consult my suite of plans and it's all there. Most public administrators realize that a good strategic plan doesn't sit on a shelf. Our plan is a working management tool forged through a living, sustainable system.

After seeing many marginal planning approaches during a career spanning over twenty five years, I now enjoy a sensible and applicable planning system. John Luthy has helped many state, city and county organizations develop strategic and operational planning systems that will enable them to be better prepared for the challenges ahead. The process described in this book helped Lincoln Public Works and Utilities develop a world-class executive management system that serves as a model for other departments in many venues. It can do the same for any public agency that is dedicated to measured performance, efficient management and continuous improvement.

This book is required reading if you are serving as an elected or appointed public official or are a career public manager or supervisor. Through both training and practical process, we are all now futurists who are serious about and actively engaged in planning for the future. Whatever comes, good planning will allow us to be better prepared for the challenges ahead. From one who has experienced a truly innovative planning approach, I encourage you to enjoy the chapters that follow and share with as many fellow public servants as you can.

— *Greg MacLean*
Director of Public Works and Utilities
City of Lincoln, Nebraska

Preface

This book is about change and challenge. It celebrates the value and creativity of public employees and their enormous contribution to society. But it is also about planning for an uncertain future. My belief is that every public official, manager, and employee must be prepared for the many escalating challenges that are now converging on our communities, not only in America, but throughout the world. Being prepared requires an interest in planning and the belief that choices made now will make a significant difference to long-term economic prosperity, social harmony and cultural stability. There is an understanding that change will occur whether we plan for it or not. And, most recognize that even if there is an investment in planning, not every plan will produce the intended results. But today, we are facing global, regional and local challenges unlike any ever encountered. Climate change, population growth, water and food shortages, terrorism, ecological destruction, resource shortages, infrastructure deterioration, and a re-centering of the world economy are all rapidly converging. It is not our nature to passively endure. More than any time in history, it is a time to review the data, identify various futures, and collaboratively chart a course toward those most preferred.

The rise and decline of strategic planning in business has been well documented. The long view, while still important, has been replaced to some extent with the admonition to 'remain adaptable and nimble,' always prepared to address the next challenge or opportunity. This advice makes sense. There has been more new information generated in the past 30 or 40 years than in the previous 5,000 and the pace of change is approaching warp speed. All the information we had available at the turn of the century will equal about one percent of what is available by 2050. Companies facing global competition must be constantly aware of new products, services, technology, and methods that could very well end their dominance or, worse, eliminate them from a competitive market.

While there has been encouragement over the past twenty-five years to manage government like a business, there are some characteristics that do not translate. Anyone who has worked in both government and business can attest to the fact that these two sectors are hugely different and, in many cases, what works for one will fail miserably in the other.

To say the least, local, state and federal government is not as nimble as business. Comparatively, change occurs at a glacial pace in government, whereas in small business the velocity of change is embraced and new products are quickly calibrated to consumer desires and capricious markets. I think of government as 'pre-framed.' For those of us who have joined a city, county or state government as new employees, the government and agency structure existed long before we became part of the workforce. For good or ill, new employees inherit structure, policies, and protocols that were most likely in place for decades. In political science, these entrenched systems are typically termed 'folkways' and define how things are done in each venue. Are these inherited systems highly adaptable to forces of change? Hardly. Joining a new business start-up is a far different proposition than joining county government. I have done both and can attest that the cultures and missions are amazingly different.

The concept of strategic thinking in public agencies is not new. Creating mission statements, identifying a vision, establishing goals, and formulating general strategies and specific actions are common elements of most plans. However, contemporary strategic thinking and planning for public agencies requires an entirely different perspective. Public agencies exist to provide services; they do not exist to generate profit for stockholders. They do not compete for markets and do not experience the win-lose environment of market competition. Some would argue that public enterprise agencies do indeed exist to generate profit; I would respond that these agencies are not competing against other service providers and additional earnings above operating costs must not far exceed the cost of providing that service or citizens would soon protest.

Ideal readers of this book understand that government exists to serve its citizens, to provide a framework for society, to ensure the desired level of public health, reasonable public transportation, safe roads, clean water, disposal of wastewater and solid waste management. It exists to protect communities against harm caused by natural or man-made disasters, crime, or social injustice. It educates our young, provides national defense, and ensures some level of security for the disadvantaged and elderly. Above all, we expect public employees to maintain the essential foundation of society, allowing citizens to pursue that elusive and very personal prize we term 'quality of life.'

During the past thirty-five years I have had the pleasure of evaluating hundreds of strategic plans prepared for city, county, state and federal agencies. Most are marginal at best. While this sounds judgmental, the genesis of my perspective has its roots in the variety of plan formats, language, and content I have seen. Most are merely aggregations of activities that are improperly termed 'goals' or 'objectives.' Many mission statements are actually visions or statements of values. Most plans provide a collage of good intentions without a clear data framework that leads to a point of departure for actual implementation and measured performance. Is this observation too harsh? Not really.

Many books on strategic planning were written by business writers who have tried to convert business planning language and process to public administration. While many terms, such as mission, values, goals, and objectives seem immune to errant interpretation, this is not the case. Some variations are subtle, others are more significant. Many of the most obvious variances were first reported in my publication, *Strategic Planning: a Guide for Public Managers*, IQ Report Volume 34, #8, published by the International City/County Management Association (ICMA) in 2002. For me, after well over three decades studying strategic thinking in the public sector and writing plans for every conceivable type of public agency, there is enormous value in standardized language and process that properly represents the specific challenges faced by *public* employees in *public* agencies.

The focus of this book is public sector strategic thinking and planning. It is dedicated to elected public officials, professional administrators, senior and middle managers, supervisors and employees who in so many profound ways are responsible for the future of our communities. I describe here a fundamental future planning perspective that is unique to government. It is a process founded on identified issues and challenges, clear data, projected outputs and desired outcomes. And, most importantly, it relies on sensible measurement and calibrated performance with a commitment to five basic operating parameters— efficiency, effectiveness, quality, productivity and cost.

There is some value in expressing what this book does *not* contain instead of a laborious review of its contents. As a child of the public sector who first mowed grass for my hometown city public works department at eighteen years of age, my perspective comes from many, many years working as an employee in state and local government, as well as from research and consulting over the past twenty-five years. This is not an academic book full of postulates, models, and arcane information that might reinforce the reader's reluctance to pursue his or her study of strategic thinking. Rather, it is a practical review of a simple planning process that actually works.

Above all, I believe in simplicity. Planning has become too complex, with too many convoluted theories and systems that rarely produce good plans in the limited time employees have available to create them. Public planning should *not* be a complex undertaking, so my ultimate desire is to share a thought process, language, sequence and general approach that can be embraced by every elected official, appointed professional manager and public employee. In this reasonably short treatment of strategic thinking and planning, I will review the following:

- The emerging world and complex challenges that now require new creative processes and solutions.

- The value of strategic thought and why public planning is unique.

- The essence of the *New Strategic Planning* and why it must be understood by every public official and administrator.

- The key elements and language of a modern public agency strategic plan.

- How plans are developed, evaluated and managed.

- Where the world seems to be evolving and why public administrators and managers at all levels must be prepared for the challenges ahead.

I state several times in this book that nothing builds a team like working collaboratively on important community issues and facing challenges together. By conducting planning as an inclusive department or community exercise, new understandings and commitments will develop. This is what excites me about sharing the process. My history and experience requires that I bring a practical, easy-to-implement approach. But it is an approach that is now well-proven and has been experienced by thousands of public employees. I think you will find it enlightening and remarkably simple.

Strategic thought, when taken as a whole, is a combination of vision, reflection, analysis, honest appraisal, and a willingness to suggest bold action. It requires dedication to look over the horizon, consider the value or possible impact of major events or situations and facilitate collaborative approaches that improve process, product, or quality of life.

Some encourage planning for its value as a means of celebrating accomplishments and contributions. Others advocate planning as a management tool that both calculates and ensures measured performance. And many practitioners would merely say strategic planning is the best means of integrating tangible current reality and projected future needs with the conceptual aspirations of a multidimensional community. All agree that good planning deals with the finite while considering the enormously diverse expectations of a nation, state, county or city. To say the least, it is important; it is vital; and it is often difficult.

Author's Note

The delight of sharing ideas and information is often diminished by those who caution the writer about time constraints, lack of real interest, been-there-done-that, and a host of other reasons to be brief and concise. I have experienced some hand-wringing over these dueling concerns. One camp is occupied by broader foundational information that creates perspective; the other insists on pure nuts-n-bolts 'how-to' instruction. Neither by itself provides the reader sufficient material to become a good strategic thinker or planner. While there are chapters dedicated to definitions, design, content and rationale, when studied in a vacuum they do not provide the underpinning that is required for current and future planning.

Therefore, I present options. Some of the best books I have read suggest a linear path through successive chapters for those who want deeper, more comprehensive knowledge and understanding. Perspective is built chapter by chapter until the reader, at the end, is more enlightened and competent. But some of these books also provide a path for those who just want to get to the essence of the subject, whether to compare notes, absorb new insight, or add another tool to the tool kit. I understand that and welcome those who merely want a book to assist with strategic plan development. For those, Parts III and IV provide a clear, detailed review of the best approach to public sector strategic plan development. Part III defines foundational plan elements, provides examples, and connects them to reality. Part IV introduces a unique planning system and way of thinking about public sector planning that ensures measurement and accountability. Part V discusses implementation, budget linkage and how to sustain quality planning year to year. For those who have considerable experience and training in strategic planning but want to explore a better way to think about public planning, going directly to Parts III or IV will save time. But, as I stress in several areas, doing so will not always answer questions pertaining to 'Why?'

Over time, I have found it best to share fundamental concepts along with their history, meaning, and value. Even a cursory overview of the concepts associated with futuring, predictability, probability and inevitability is helpful. Especially for administrators, managers and elected officials who have never studied political science, community development, economic development, comprehensive planning and many related fields, the background will be invaluable. For those who just want to get to the section on plan development, I would encourage you to glean what you can and use it to your best advantage. But when you have both time and inclination, return to the earlier chapters to gain a deeper understanding and broader perspective that will forever change how you think about and plan for the future of your community.

*If you don't know where you're going,
any path will take you there.*

—Sioux Proverb

Part One

Thinking About *The Future*

What is more important than the future? While the past is interesting and can serve as a reference point for future generations, it does not necessarily dictate what comes next. It has been said that, to become wise, one must have been unwise. Any historical review will illuminate a vast number of unwise acts, poor decisions, and the absence of foresight. As we contemplate the decades ahead, it would seem clear that we will be challenged to understand what is at stake and the various consequences of both action and inaction. With the predicted global population approaching nine billion by 2050, the clash of ideologies and search for natural resources to fuel economic growth, maintain mobility, and feed the masses will become classic pivot points for both cooperation and conflict. Whether or not societies enter a new era of collaboration depends on their individual and collective worldview regarding what is both possible and preferred.

The most valued questions virtually always pertain to the future...what it portends, how it can be modified by actions taken in the present, and what will happen IF? Elected officials, public administrators and managers at every level are being asked to look forward; they are being encouraged to peer into an uncertain future and make decisions that will have enormous impact on subsequent generations. Is that new city hall, jail, library, school, bridge, courthouse, port, airport runway, levee, or fire station a wise decision based on available information? Will it add to quality of life, economic vitality, social harmony, public safety, and cultural equality? Will it produce ongoing contributions and positive consequences for the greater community? Do the benefits outweigh the detriments? And, of course, how and when will you know?

What about inaction? With a re-centering economy and budgets growing more restricted, should deferred maintenance continue for so many roads, water and wastewater systems, sidewalks, schools, airports, ports, and fleets? Should you continue to defer upgrades to security, record keeping, and computer systems? And, perhaps most critical, should you continue to reduce training and professional development at a time when public employees need to be at the top of their game in terms of efficiency, quality and productivity?

The following three chapters introduce a discussion about possibility, probability, predictability and inevitability. Throughout Part I, my premise is straightforward...elected officials and public administrators are futurists who must embrace the predictive aspect of their work. It is an emerging perspective, but one that must gain greater attention in the years ahead. No longer can public managers afford to focus all their energies on daily operations and plans that accommodate annual budget requests. A growing portion of public leadership must now be concentrated on understanding and planning for various potential and predicted futures. Because futuring is both art and science, it requires expanded vision and a willingness to confront reality, assess risk, and seek the best possible community outcomes. Based on the evidence, it would appear that many futures are indeed predictable.

After reading these three chapters, I would hope that you find this to be true and that you, too, are indeed a futurist who is properly positioned to address the many challenges and opportunities to come.

Chapter 1

The Future and Public Leadership

A few years ago, I was presenting at the American Public Works Association International Congress and had an opportunity to work with David Zach, a talented and entertaining futurist speaker. My program later that afternoon was on the future of public works and addressed challenges leaders would face. One area where David and I differ relates to the concept of predictability.

Even as a trained futurist, David's stated view that day was that the future is not foreseeable and it is folly to attempt prediction. Later, during my program I may have broken protocol by disagreeing with that perspective. While there are certainly many outlying 'Black Swans' and related variables that will have impacts that are impossible to predict, there are many more that have measurable and predictable outcomes. Public leaders need to explore and understand many converging trends and be committed to planning for predictable community impact. Remember, much of history is cyclic—it repeats itself...you just have to understand the history, be aware of critical trends and have the foresight to implement ahead of the curve. Much of what goes around *does* come around. The message is simply, pay attention and you will be much better prepared.

Yes, You *Are* a Futurist!

Comments above notwithstanding, without reservation I concur that much of the future is unpredictable. However, from a planner's viewpoint, given the correct data, we can predict many things. Why do I say this? Let me relate a short story.

During a program I presented to a group of highly technical public employees, an engineer quite heatedly expressed his frustration with the program, stating that predicting the future was impossible and that I was wasting their time. I asked his permission to explore his view through a series of simple questions. Reluctantly, he agreed. I proceeded to ask him the following questions:

Question 1: In your community, if the population grows by 30% over the next decade, do you think water consumption will increase, decline or remain the same? He replied that water consumption would probably rise.

Question 2: If the population increases by 30% in that same time period, do you think that, without any new alternatives, traffic congestion in the city core will increase or decrease? He replied that it would most likely increase. By then, there was a faint change in his demeanor.

Question 3: With the increased traffic, would you say that street surfaces and reflective striping will deteriorate faster, slower or at about the same rate? By then, he was squirming a bit but answered that roads and streets and various painted surfaces would probably deteriorate faster.

I looked at him and, with some drama said, "Well, you *can* predict the future!" Along with some laughter, there was obviously renewed vigor among participants. Being a good sport, he joined in an active discussion about how knowledge and data can drive predictability in many areas of public management. Within a few minutes, the audience had grasped the basis of my belief about the value of predictability. As populations grow, we can predict an increase in service demand—more licenses, building permits, immunizations, inspections, water use, solid waste and waste water generated, etc. We can also predict detrimental impact—if water supplies are contaminated (potential for cholera, typhoid), restaurants are not inspected (food poisoning via salmonella, e-coli) or immunization levels drop below 65% among children in the K–3rd grade age group (epidemics of preventable childhood disease, such as diphtheria, whooping cough, measles and mumps). Those in law enforcement can provide equations proven accurate over time that reflect the need for more patrol officers, more jail cells, correctional officers and even more judges if a city or county expands significantly. History provides sound health, epidemiological, engineering, public safety, administrative and other data that, in the right combination, promotes predictability.

The point I am making is that it takes a change in *perspective* to become a strategic thinker and futurist. As public leaders and managers begin to blend their tendency to 'operationalize' every aspect of government with a process of strategic thought, they will gain an entirely new ability to predict, plan and budget for predictable and already known events. Those who argue that the future is unpredictable forget that forecasting occurs annually as budgets are being prepared. The level of predictive expertise and foresight in public agencies is enormous. It merely has to be tapped.

A New Era

There is currently a great deal of discussion about *change*. It seems clear to me that change is what occurs in the normal course of economic, social and biological evolution—it occurs regardless of what we do. In every era there are big changes and small changes. Some are profound, most are not. My best guess is that we are entering a new era; from all appearances it is a time of transition and transformation. Predictions range from the end of the world in December 2012 (according to the Mayan calendar) to the death of industrialization and devolution into a global agrarian society within a hundred years. We read predictions of the United States being divided into four autonomous mega regions, China eclipsing the U.S. as the global economic power and about worldwide class, economic or religious warfare. Those things are hard to predict...but there are *a lot* of capable people dedicated to positive outcomes related to climate, economics, peace, and global collaboration. For every negative possible future, there is a positive future. For virtually every negative variable, there is a counter-trend. However, change is in

For every negative possible future, there is an alternative positive future.

the air. Tipping points have been reached in several areas and, you can be assured, the pace of change will soon accelerate. The outcomes could be profound.

The Concept of *Legacy*

I first began to write about the value of 'legacy' for public leaders and managers over twenty years ago. My premise was then and remains that nothing is more important than the legacy one leaves behind after a period of public service. The state, city or county will go on. It was there before we employees arrived and will most likely be there after we move on. So, the critical questions for each reader are, 'What will you leave behind? Will the organization be more efficient? Have you implemented new processes that are now a part of the culture? Is there more support, understanding, and credibility relative to public services? Is the community safer, more prosperous or more harmonious?'

Strategic thinkers always have an eye on the horizon. While considering and planning for current events and circumstances, there is a parallel focus on possible futures. In many ways, there are three distinct areas that public leaders must consider:

- Current realities that require a focus on maintaining current operations;

- A vision of the future that reflects the mission, beliefs and desires of the agency, government and community;

- Possible and predicted events that will drive decision-making, fund allocation, and priority setting in the years to come.

The level of predictive expertise and foresight in public agencies is enormous…it merely has to be tapped.

When properly aligned, vision, analysis, planning and dogged implementation provide the essential underpinning for *Legacy*. The legacy we leave greatly depends on how we perceive, plan for, and address predicted events, as well as those that are currently impacting and will inevitably converge on our communities in the future (an aging population, for instance).

Government Failures

Most Americans are in denial. From all appearances, many people believe that, with a little luck and a few stimulus dollars, things will soon return to the 'good old days.' Others predict a longer return to 'normal' citing an inherent inclination toward innovation and the creative American spirit as forces that will right the ship. In most ways, this is not going to happen—at least not the 'return to the good old days' part. That is not to say that the future will be a dark, gloomy and bankrupt place with few opportunities and rampant cultural decline. It merely means that the planet is different, resource levels are lower, connectivity is greater, and what worked well from 1950 through 2010 may not work so well in the years to come. Let's just say it's a new day...a new era, and government at all levels *must* provide leadership. To accomplish this, several things must be done:

- Government leaders and managers *must* become more enlightened about converging trends that will bring enormous community change.

- These same leaders and managers must understand the difference between issue and *impact*; change doesn't matter much unless it has **impact**. What are the potential impacts of known trends and predicted changes?

- Government must become more collaborative and share a longer view; impact and opportunity will encompass *regions*—not just communities. How can we engender a new commitment to regional cooperation and consolidation?

- At all levels, public leaders and managers must become more aware of escalating issues and challenges; government must be more adaptable and nimble when addressing known or predicted events. This takes leadership—not politics.

- Inertia is eroding the democratic process. There is gridlock everywhere. Dark and potentially radical changes will take place when health care bankrupts more families, education is affordable only for children of the rich, and gasoline is $6 or $8 per gallon.

When it takes $100 to fill the gas tank, perhaps then we'll see more support for alternative energy, conservation, and oil exploration. With peak oil now an openly discussed, data-driven fact, how long will it take to address the 'what ifs' related to reduced oil supplies and $6 gas? Same with climate change and potential for drought in key agricultural regions, reduced mineral supplies, and eroding infrastructure. In this book, I won't even get into education, Social Security, Medicaid and Medicare costs or the general health care debate. However, when I speak of converging variables, all of these will dramatically impact community life as we know it. The common interests of every community must replace politics as the dominant force for positive change.

- We must deal with fundamental issues—many related to economics, finance and business—but others related to 'first things first.' What are the basic human and community needs that provide the foundation for quality of life, prosperity, and economic vitality? Never mind that there may be a notable contraction in the *size* of local economies—at least for a period of time; people can still prosper and have a great life with much less. Does anyone doubt that?

Confronting a Common Foe

I take every opportunity to encourage government leaders to **'Confront Reality!'** The common foe is not change; it is the unwillingness to confront issues and pose tough remedies. Oceans will rise, the planet will continue to warm, the global population will grow, oil and other natural resources will be depleted, and cultures will compete. It is the historic cycle. The most critical questions

At all levels, public leaders and managers must become more aware of escalating issues and challenges; government must be more adaptable and nimble when addressing known or predicted events. This takes leadership—not politics.

pertain to our response and willingness to make a commitment to a future legacy. Government is being overwhelmed; converging challenges are just too big. Regardless, like it or not, a new transformative era is underway and gaining momentum. The real work begins with every state and local community and, as strategic thinkers, there is much we can analyze, predict and address. It's time for every community to confront the evolving world and pursue thoughtful strategies that forge new alliances and promising new paths to desired alternative futures. There are options and opportunities.

But, do we have the vision, competitive spirit and will to collaboratively work through each complex issue? And will we do so before it is too late?

Chapter 2

The New Futurists – Public Administrators and Elected Officials

I can already hear the comments, 'What is he thinking!? We're not futurists! Strategic planners perhaps, but what is this *futurist* stuff?'

As mentioned earlier, I believe that every elected official, manager and administrator is, in his or her own way, a futurist who can and will inadvertently gather adequate data to develop significant foresight about the future. I encourage you to be open to that idea. Some public managers are already quite active in forecasting and preparing for future challenges. Forecasting is an annual event for water, wastewater and solid waste managers. It is common for police and fire departments to forecast needs based on projected crime, social change, emergency response or emerging public safety needs. Public health departments forecast immunization levels, laboratory, clinic, environmental health, and inspection requirements based on demographic data and trend analysis. However, for most, providing forecasts for annual budget requests is far different than accepting the label of 'futurist.' Actually, they are not that dissimilar. As I've said, it is a matter of perception and perspective.

Considering the Future

The thing about the future is that, just because we take time to look at it, we assume our review will somehow change it. Subtly, with direct action, or inadvertently through the power of suggestion, we'll alter it. Why?

Because outcomes are never secure no matter how much we plan and analyze. But they are altered because we tried or avoided, or prioritized, or allocated more effort toward various remedies.

My focus has always been on the future. One summer years ago, while in basic Army training at Ft. Polk, Louisiana, I recall that I intently focused on the date of graduation in late September. If you have ever done physically demanding work or training in the Louisiana summer, you'll have some understanding of why I focused on the projected endpoint. Thankfully, I made it and was rewarded by being sent for training to Ft. Sam Houston and Brooke Army Hospital (later changed to Medical Center) in San Antonio. Although it was also blessed with that fierce south Texas warmth, by then it was approaching fall and I was in a beautiful city.

The relevance of this experience became more apparent as years passed. Every day that elapses is gone forever. Today is the present and yesterday is the past. While the past is interesting and a wonderland of experience (even at Ft. Polk) the future is where we are all going to live. Public leaders, perhaps more than any other category of managers, must have this perspective. Why? Because we rely on them to have a vision, analyze what is best, make sensible plans, and properly implement those plans.

While recent polls might indicate otherwise, in America we have always trusted our leaders. They have historically been seen as having the best interest of the community as the centerpiece of every decision. Those of you who are elected or appointed public leaders or who lead from senior management positions hold much of the future in your hands. Focus on it; keep your eye on the horizon and on the many horizons you encounter; care about the future and consider it in every decision you make. That is the foundation and substance of *legacy*.

Assessing the Possibilities

As a thinker about the future, there are several questions that belong in your tool kit. The first involves how to generate ideas about possible futures. Don't be afraid to ask about the *potential* for an event to occur or a situation to arise. What is the potential for the population to increase, traffic congestion to grow, immunization rates to fall, or economic development to decline by 20%? If the population grows, how will it affect your agency or program? What is the likelihood that you will have to serve more people, handle more transactions, or open more facilities? A strategic thinker is constantly looking for trends that will offer some indication that change will occur—or *not* occur.

The clarity and simplicity of strategic planning, along with support from employees and stakeholders will depend to a great extent on viable data that illuminates various possibilities. These can be either beneficial or detrimental to the organization, state or community. The key question is, 'What does the data tell you about the potential that an event might or *might not* occur?' Remember, it is just as important to consider the potential of a *desired event* not actually happening as to consider the potential of a negative event or situation actually happening.

Public leaders and managers must be not only willing but *interested* in and *committed* to scanning the horizon for positive and negative possibilities that will impact the community. When working with public administrators and elected officials, I look for, or attempt to produce, eight characteristics that are important to possibility assessment:

1. A natural curiosity about the broader world and a natural worldview.

2. Leaders and managers who are well-read and in touch with current events.

3. Courage to pose difficult questions about where the agency, community or government is going.

4. An appreciation for the past but a focus on the future.

5. Interest in the ideas and suggestions of others; open to new concepts and possibilities.

6. Willingness to actually try something new and to change direction if needed.

7. An interest in and appreciation for data and data analysis, and the courage to ask 'What does this mean?'

8. An understanding that while some things are not predictable, there are many things about future events that *are* predictable.

For those contemplating who to promote or appoint to a strategic position, I recommend these (and other) characteristics. Possibility is related to vision wherein one might ask, 'What are the possibilities for this state, community, or organization to achieve greatness?' In addition to exploring bold, encompassing visions, strategic thinkers must also ask 'What is the possibility that X might occur and how do we prepare for that eventuality?'

A strategic thinker is constantly looking for trends that will offer some indication that change will occur — or not occur.

Predictability

Traditional forecasting using mathematical models takes public managers in the wrong direction and creates frustrations that reduce their willingness to participate in planning. In my view, it is better to use geology, material science, demographics and a variety of If-Then scenarios based on empirical evidence *and* knowledge/intuition about the subject. Let's take material science as one example.

Asphalt road surfaces are made from composite material engineered to bear huge vehicle loads, withstand extremes of heat and cold, hold painted reflective material, and endure rugged use for long periods with little maintenance. Material scientists specializing in road surfaces have calibrated, through years of testing and experimentation, various formulas that will work in virtually any condition on the planet. Public works and transportation professionals, mostly civil engineers and highly trained road surface and materials technicians, are well-schooled in these formulas and can calibrate them to state, city and county needs. They don't need complicated probability calculations to determine how long road surfaces will last if they know traffic and weather patterns, and track other variables as they occur. From experience, they also know proper maintenance schedules and how to maintain road surfaces to maximize longevity and durability.

Here's the point: Public leaders and administrators must be able to predict potential outcomes in order to effectively forecast maintenance, operating budgets, and other unintended events that may or may not occur. With proper training and perspective, public employees are perfectly positioned to make fairly accurate predictions and calculate probability without complex formulas and exercises that generally get them no closer to an accurate prediction.

Some tools worth considering (and generally already used through a serendipitous approach) include:

- **Expert forecasting** – Use the talents and experience of those on staff who have been well-trained and have years dealing with the issue. This method can be merged with convening a team of experts who establish a shared system of trial and feedback.

- **Structured analogies** – Comparisons with other state, city and county organizations who have similar experiences and can share results (public agencies are great because they generally share everything).

- **Decomposition** – Deconstruct what has occurred historically, to understand what happened, why, and what can be done differently. There is an invaluable 'laboratory' for every application and circumstance.

- **Judgment and experimentation** – Using the combined education, training and experience of key parties, allow them to identify, analyze and solve problems and establish new protocols.

- **Statistical analysis** – An important element of operations that should be incorporated into every aspect of government agencies. Uses data-driven measurement and continuous feedback to improve systems and approaches.

What is the Probability?

Once we have considered the variety of potential events and circumstances that *might* impact the organization or community, it is important to evaluate the *probability* that they will occur. These are two very different factors in the equation. One is a summation of what is possible; the other is a calculation that will indicate the chance that it will actually occur.

As suggested in the Author's Notes, much of probability theory and its arcane mathematical formulae is unnecessary and generally a waste of time for public leaders and administrators. Unless one has a deep interest and compelling drive to employ sophisticated mathematical formulas to assist with probability, I would suggest other methods.

For the sake of discussion, however, (and to accommodate those who are math whizzes) I enjoy reviewing complex formulas that verify or disprove a prediction. Much of discrete probability theory deals with events such as throwing dice, experiments with playing cards, and other acts of randomness. Those more prone to experimentation would use a formula that calculates the probability of an event based on the number of times it typically occurs over the potential number of possible outcomes. For the purpose of providing sensible government services and preparing for future challenges, we are interested in *what* might occur and the *potential* of it occurring within a prescribed time period. There are many formulas available to assist with calculating probability. The International Institute of Forecasting has guidelines and a wealth of formulas available. I use hardly any. Why? Because they don't tell me what I need to know.

Public leaders and administrators are seasoned futurists who must be able to predict potential outcomes in order to effectively forecast maintenance needs, operating budgets, and other unintended events that may or may not occur.

Probability vs. Predictability

While some may see minimal distinctions between these two aspects of forecasting, there are nuanced variations worth noting. For public administrators and elected officials, it is important to accept the value of predictability – understanding that it is indeed possible to predict and forecast many events or circumstances that will occur in the distant or near future.

Predictability in this context is the ability to review empirical data, historic outcomes and trend patterns, then aggregate with a variety of expert wisdom to elicit a belief that something will occur. Whether a startling event (bridge collapse) or a situation (falling immunization rates), the right mix of information and expertise can result in a reasonable prediction that *if* conditions do not change, the predicted event will most likely occur.

Probability then becomes the *extent* to which we believe the event or situation will occur, when it might occur, and the calculated *probability* associated with it actually happening *ever* or in the time period predicted. Rudimentarily, a senior manager might ask, 'On a one to ten scale, what is the probability that the levee will rupture if we get a sustained five inches of rain and high winds over a 24-hour period?' The response will be governed by a combination of engineering expertise, experience, data (soil/fill composition, compaction, height, base width, structure age, etc.) and historic comparisons to other areas that endured similar situations. The same would be true of a bridge judged substandard and at-risk. What is the potential for it to collapse? What is the probability it will do so within the next five years? What variables will increase/reduce that probability? Managers must ask two related questions: What can we predict that might occur? And, what is the probability that it will actually occur? There might be a third question, which is, what can we do to change that probability and, if nothing else, buy more time?

Is it Inevitable?

As forward-looking strategic thinkers, public administrators and elected officials must continually ask: 'What are the possibilities? What is the potential for something to happen? What can we predict? What is the probability of this occurring?

It is also essential to understand what is *inevitable*. Very simply, this means that a complete plan must consider factors and forces that are already in motion. We know they will occur and will have impact. For example, Baby Boomers have already been born and are aging. Close to 78 million Boomers growing older will have a significant impact on Social Security, Veterans hospitals, long-term care, health care, Medicaid, Medicare, etc. We don't have to wonder *if* this group will impact these systems—it is inevitable that it will. Leadership questions do not address *if* this will occur; they are concerned with *how* this inevitable force will influence costs, service delivery, funding levels, priorities, voting, etc.

What other forces are already in play that will affect your state or local community? What systems have been constructed that must be maintained? The national highway system, the Internet, thousands of bridges and dams, and thousands of miles of sidewalks, water mains and levees are already in place. Their aging process and maintenance requirements are not potential—they are inevitable. Give this some thought. From your vantage point, what are the known forces that will change your community? What will it cost to maintain, educate, repair, upgrade, support, or satisfy?

Inevitability is an integral part of scenario planning, which is addressed in more depth in another book in the *Public Leadership* series.

Impact and Magnitude

Much of this book is dedicated to a simple, straightforward strategic thinking and planning approach that is unique to public agencies. A central attribute of this system is a foundation that requires identification of critical external and internal issues that now—or will someday—impact the organization, citizens, or the greater community. However, an essential question for planners relates to the level of impact each issue or challenge will have. A common theme throughout this book concerns the ability to assess value. If an event occurs but has little impact, or its impact is narrowly focused, it may not deserve a high priority, especially during fiscally constrained periods like the one I believe will continue for much of the coming decade 2010–2020.

Is magnitude predictable? I have found that in many situations the probability that impact will be high, moderate or low can be calculated based on data, experience, or comparisons with similar events. A bridge collapse during rush hour, a city-wide whooping cough epidemic in the K-6 school population, a forest fire in a heavily logged national forest, and the impact of rapid population growth on a small city water system, will all have significant impact. The magnitude will be modified in some cases depending on other variables, such as time of day (bridge collapse), immunization levels (whooping cough epidemic during the school year), or the advent of sustained heavy rain (scope of the forest fire).

Impact is most often assessed *after* the fact, as in the aftermath of the 2010 Haiti earthquake. Public safety officials and United Nations advisors had stressed for years over shoddy construction throughout the country. While the earthquake was not especially predictable, the enormous level of death and destruction from a major quake was highly probable and, in this case, inevitable once the event occurred.

A less potent example might be a water line rupture in a downtown city core. Due to the age of water mains in many U.S. cities, breaks are predictable, highly probable and inevitable. Experience has demonstrated that a sizeable downtown water main break will have significant impact on traffic, commerce, budgets and public sentiment. A water main break of equal size in an outlying neighborhood that has few businesses, little traffic and fewer residents might frustrate those citizens but overall community impact will be minimal.

Magnitude and Intensity

It seems clear that good planning requires identifying current problems and prospective issues along with an assessment of potential magnitude and impact. But elected officials and executive level managers must also consider factors that contribute to *intensity*. Whereas magnitude might address the breadth of the event, intensity relates to how intense the damage (or impact) is in one location or to one segment of the population.

Public health planners are quite aware that the magnitude of a measles epidemic might be great because there are reported cases in 100% of area schools. However, *intensity* relates to how many children are out sick in a given school. If one school is experiencing a 10% absenteeism rate due to the disease, but another school has 35% of children absent due to sickness, one could say that the event is more intense in the school with the higher rate. What contributed to that intensity? Is it just bad luck? Is it due to immunization levels in that school? Are there different preventive standards? Public health professionals study causative factors that contribute to potential, probability, and likely impact, with attention paid to *both* magnitude and intensity. Similar discussions should be (and are generally) held among those dealing with physical infrastructure, social services, utilities, fire, police, etc. Let's face it, a bridge collapse on a remote rural road at 3 AM will be less intense than a similar event occurring in the middle of rush hour in a downtown city core. Of course, the rural bridge collapse will still be seen as quite intense for the unfortunate driver who just happened to be in the wrong place at the wrong time!

Strategic thinkers ask questions. Given the data and, based on your experience, what might happen? What is the probability of it occurring? If the event does occur, or the prospective situation arises, what can you predict about its magnitude? Will it have significant impact and if so, to whom? Could the impact be highly intense in some areas and not in others? Where and why might that variance occur?

Discounting Probability

Imagine that there are those who are complacent about predicted or even highly probable events (yes, imagine that!). Residents of San Francisco know there was a significant earthquake (estimated at 7.7 to 8.25 on the Richter scale) on April 18, 1906 that resulted in tremendous destruction. They also know the city is highly susceptible to quakes due to its position adjacent to the San Andreas Fault. Other than the Loma Prieta earthquake that occurred in the San Francisco area in 1989, there have been no other serious quakes in northern California for over a hundred years, so the current level of daily (or even occasional) concern seems minimal.

Being a serious thought leader in the areas of probability and strategic planning, consider the impact of *stability* on motivation, awareness, and concern. Those who study predictability are faced with a huge psychological barrier that often precludes any progress toward preemptive action. Stability or repetition over time can lead to the belief that randomness is tamed and probability is deeply discounted. That is, the situation is no longer a relevant issue or worse, is less probable than originally thought. There are also those who respond by saying, 'Oh well...we can't do anything about it, so I might as well just live my life and hope for the best.' Even though the official (and fabricated) 1906 death toll was placed at only 379, research since then has placed the actual number of deaths at over 3,000. Most of the buildings in the city today were rebuilt in the first half of the 20th Century to old and very lax building codes, allowing many of the replaced buildings to be no better than those destroyed in 1906. Current predictions state that an earthquake even close to the 1906 level would destroy many areas of the city and leave thousands dead. So... is there any remote potential of such an event recurring and is it probable? Is such an event generally predictable? Not the timing of the event, but the occurrence of the future event itself?

If there are no disease outbreaks, Category 5 hurricanes, F5 tornados (Fujita scale), contaminated water supplies or total failure of the waste treatment plant, the potential for a serious event carries less weight over time. This occurs even though over the same period all pertinent data and historic evidence indicates higher, not lower, probability and even greater impact if/when it actually occurs. During the past hundred years, the development of San Francisco has been enormous. Does anyone doubt that, when the next earthquake occurs, the impact will be catastrophic? The same is true when there are no epidemics over a long period. People begin to rationalize the value of immunizations or the importance of carefully monitored water systems. In virtually every discipline, reduced standards and complacency tend to follow long periods without major events.

This is dangerous, but it is an element of the human condition...the mind rationalizes, explains, discounts and easily accepts 'assumed norms' based on the absence over time of serious negative events. Various groups in the community will begin questioning the value of building restrictions, immunizations, food testing, water treatment, pipe replacement, or expansion of emergency services. Even though data and experience tell us (and the Centers for Disease Control reminds us) that immunization rates for childhood disease must remain above 80 to 85% to preclude epidemics in school populations, rates continue to fluctuate. Worse, if immunization levels fall and no epidemics occur, many begin to question the data's validity and the program's value vs. it's cost. This has already occurred in many areas, not only related to immunizations but also pertaining to a variety of programs dedicated to poison prevention, consumer protection, street repair, building codes, infrastructure replacement, drug treatment, community policing, and other vital public services.

It often takes the unfortunate event—a serious epidemic, a bridge collapse, an earthquake, or other highly probable outcome with the potential for death, disability and economic disaster—to again affirm the original, proven value of preventive measures. The worst situations may be those with more subtle impacts, such as the low, almost imperceptible growth in crime when drug treatment and other social service programs are reduced or eliminated. Subtle impacts are far more difficult to counter than sudden catastrophic events.

However, major unexpected events can disrupt entire economies, destroy ecosystems, and alter cultures. A sad but potent example of magnitude and intense impact is the April 20, 2010 explosion of British Petroleum's Deepwater Horizon oil rig and subsequent catastrophic oil leakage that has affected so much of the Gulf Coast. Without doubt, there are significant challenges associated with deepwater drilling and a certain amount of probability can be calculated into disaster planning. In this case, not only did 11 employees lose their lives, coastal cities, counties and states are trying to contend with catastrophic ecological contamination that may ultimately destroy a centuries-old fishing industry and debilitate a potent tourism industry. All the factors were present: probability of a negative event, the potential of huge impact, enormous intensity and an undercurrent of complacency enabled by a history of few disastrous deepwater well events.

Strategic thinkers must keep in mind that **if** the probability of the event is high and the magnitude of its impact is significant (as determined by those with the expertise *and* the power to relay a potent message), then the risk is too great to neglect preemptive action. Unfortunately, complacency is produced by long periods without serious impact from potential events, so a 'deferred maintenance' or avoidance culture develops, often with disastrous consequences. Or, as suggested above, services or reviews are incrementally reduced with no obvious impact, prompting more cuts until a tipping point is reached and major impact occurs. Even if such impact is delayed, the community ultimately suffers and a return to equilibrium often takes many years.

Because human beings tend to worry too late and plan too little, preparations are often wholly inappropriate for the magnitude of the potential event. So, the question lingers: how can we efficiently maximize preparation while not obsessing over all the potential consequences? There is no easy answer. The key is crafting plans that identify critical issues, state their potential impact and offer thoughtful (and preemptive) goals, strategies and action plans.

In virtually every discipline, reduced standards and complacency tend to follow long periods without major events.

The role of public leaders becomes very important when there is an indication that complacency could blind entire communities to potential disaster. This is not a 'Chicken Little' phenomenon. This is planning for events that have enormous consequences yet are ignored or avoided by citizens. Pay attention, share data, and encourage discussions about impact. Above all, have the courage to maintain standards that, to the extent possible, moderate negative impact while promoting growth, health, safety, security and economic vitality.

Myopic Limitations

Public agencies are limited by an annual budget culture (some are biennial) that restricts the ability to get very far outside the proverbial fiscal box. As a result, department directors spend an inordinate amount of time fiddling with budgets while the world around them is evolving at breakneck speed. Needs are shifting, priorities are in flux, demand is escalating, and economic realities are constricting both options and the will to amend. Am I discounting the need to attend to budgets? No. I am merely encouraging a balance between operations planning and strategic thought.

Although I am burdened with the tendency to repeat, I am driven to my redundant nature by the concern that insufficient attention is being paid to future challenges. There is an amazing predilection among elected public officials and administrators to limit predictions to the next annual cycle and even then address only what can be presented in the budget. I rant (mildly), cajole, and otherwise attempt to encourage public officials and managers to consider *both* the acceptable budget and program-

continuing aspects of annual requests, as well as the multidimensional
requirements of potential futures.

Today, while taking a break from writing, I visited with a colleague who
declared that few managers or elected officials in state and local
government dedicate enough time to future planning. With statutes
requiring balanced budgets, state governments are deeply engaged in
current fiscal issues, generally related to what can be reduced or
eliminated to save money. City and county governments are experiencing
similar circumstances. Based on trend analysis and my personal beliefs,
for several years (probably 2009 through 2013 and perhaps beyond)
revenue will be too low in some cities, counties and states to maintain
current operations—even at 2007 or 2008 levels. Unfortunately, demand
has not diminished and in fact has increased, due to more people seeking
government financial, medical, and social services. Population has also
continued to grow. Basic services associated with transportation, public
health, fire protection, police and corrections, courts support
administration (grounds, buildings, security, information technology,
purchasing, building inspection, permitting, assessment, and many
others) are still required general government services. And of course, in
most states and municipalities, education funding consumes far more
resources than any other government program.

It would seem plausible that, due to growing disconnects between
funding and service demand, more rather than less attention would be
paid to future issues and challenges.
Instead, the genesis of a bunker mentality *It often takes the unfortunate*
may have been created with the Great *event – a serious epidemic, a*
Recession of 2008–2009. Unfortunately, *bridge collapse, an*
failure to forge an even stronger focus on *earthquake, or other highly*
the future will bring more negatives than *probable outcome with the*
the attention being paid to current *potential for death, disability*
budgets and the act of somehow grinding *and economic disaster to*
through each successive and similar *again affirm the original,*
budget season. *proven value of preventive*
measures.

The real issue here is that myopic
predictions of the future are limited predictions. They do not promote
adequate attention or commitment to confront pending or anticipated

realities. While potentially huge outcomes can be predicted and will only become more likely and potent if inaction continues, we see elected officials, managers and administrators conscientiously diddle with smaller, less controversial and more convenient issues and their associated activities. Somehow, we must take the long view; officials and managers must promote dual track planning that allows focus on meaningful operations while also identifying critical issues and challenges that could capsize the entire system. Some events are foreseeable, others aren't. But, to neglect potential circumstances and events and avoid preparing for them can be much more devastating than reduced budget dollars.

Parallel Perspectives

In the current financial environment, with similar conditions predicted for another half-decade or more, parallel perspectives are required. One addresses the need to balance planning for current operations against strategic plans that pledge assets against serious predictable (or inevitable) issues that have a high likelihood of occurring. The second perspective is driven by the need to counter the program-centric mentality reflected in the tendency to circle the wagons when dollars get tight. Many program managers admit to less joint planning and collaboration when programs enter the survival zone. There are often enormous consequences from an erosion of collaborative planning once it becomes "every man for himself."

In virtually every alternate future that can be envisioned by a review of trends and historic experience, there will be multiple outcomes that will impact *multiple* agencies. There were those who analyzed, believed, then reported the potential that Louisiana's 630-sq-mi Lake Pontchartrain levees would fail, given circumstances associated with Category 4 and 5 hurricanes. Analysis and concerns were outlined in more than one If-Then situation analyses. However, many agencies (and people) were *not* indicated in these reports, yet were hugely affected by this one disastrous event. Education, health, social services, police, fire/rescue, EMS, public transportation, public works, utilities, and dozens of other agencies were overwhelmed by the event known as Hurricane Katrina. However, it would appear that predictions were not nearly as multidimensional or inclusive as they should have been. While many agencies worked in great harmony and collaborated on planning and service delivery, if all agencies had prior involvement with predictions regarding both the *potential* of the event and the *impact* afterward, preemptive action might have prevailed enough to avert a national crisis.

There are always multiple outcomes to predicted and non-predicted events. Myopic planning and predicting does not embrace a large enough community of responders, providers, and citizens. The admonition is simple. The required multidimensional perspective must be driven by public leaders who ask tough questions about impact and invite the broadest possible participant base to the table. They must also have a dual focus on both near- and long-term budgeting, ensuring that key efforts that address predicted scenarios are funded along with current operations.

Engineers as Models

Engineers make great planners once they get past difficulties with the concept of futuring and predicting the future. From experience with many engineers in both private and public organizations, I would contend that their work often provides the underpinning (sometimes literally) to strategic thought as it pertains to predictability. Very simply, we trust engineers to analyze the best possible means to accomplish tangible ends. We ask them to plan, construct and maintain water supply systems, road systems, waste treatment plants, parks, and buildings of every shape, size and purpose. We trust that they will conduct the proper research, analysis, and calculations before rendering technical advice regarding the potential success of an intended project. Having worked with engineers and technicians for many years, I can honestly say I have rarely heard or read of a positive or negative recommendation that was not grounded in fact or did not have merit. To be sure, 'over-engineering' is occasionally an issue, but recommendations generally pursue predictable outcomes driven by thoughtful review and hard fact.

I use engineers as an example due to their penchant for 'provability.' Most of us have heard homilies about the wisdom of not building a house on sand (or on an unstable tectonic fault line). We can carry that metaphor further: Don't build a house on a cliff made of soft soil with no associated bedrock that is subject to high wind, considerable rain and potentially high waves. We have seen news video of such homes collapsing due to eroded soil and failed foundations because of those very factors. The same might be said for those who build in steep canyons prone to dry season fire danger and mudslides during heavy spring rains. There are many who are on record as having warned those homeowners and builders of the variables that could potentially converge to bring disastrous consequences. Whether discussing buildings, levees, roads, bridges, waste and water treatment plants, watershed management, parks, or any other aspect of public service, engineering considers data, scientific research and proven technology to answer questions about the possibility of failure, insufficient capacity, or eroded capability, and the probability, impact, magnitude, and intensity of any potential event.

Complacency is produced by long periods without serious impact from potential events, so a 'deferred maintenance' or avoidance culture develops…often with disastrous consequences.

Another example might be helpful. The Cascadia subduction zone is a 680-mile-long fault located approximately 50 miles off the Pacific Northwest coast. It is where the Juan de Fuca plate curves beneath the North American continent. Though inactive for over 300 years, there are signs, as there are with the San Andreas Fault, that pressures are building as the plate continues its easterly slide. Based on data simulations and forensic evidence, we know that the earthquake that occurred in 1700 was a magnitude–9 and caused 30 to 40 foot high tsunami waves all along the Northwest Pacific coast. Research collected at Oregon State University by the Active Tectonics and Seafloor Mapping Laboratory indicates an 80% chance the southern end of the fault off southern Oregon and Northern California will break in the next 50 years, generating a mega quake.

In 2001 a 6.8 magnitude earthquake centered in Olympia, Washington caused significant damage but resulted in no deaths. It did draw more attention to the potential of a similar or stronger quake and that the probability of a very powerful event is growing. The Associated Press has reported that Oregon has 1,300 schools and public safety buildings that are at 'high risk' of collapsing during a major earthquake. State law requires that all public safety structures that are in jeopardy of collapsing during a major quake must be upgraded by 2022 and all public schools by

2032. With tight budgets and the tendency to defer maintenance while tending to immediate operating requirements, can this possibly be accomplished? We have the technical data, it has happened before (when the population was virtually zero), and there are recent and very real examples of what happens IF (earthquakes in Haiti and Chile). It is a form of Russian Roulette that seems destined to have disastrous consequences.

Given proper perspective, data, and experience prediction. is possible. While magnitude and intensity may not always be fully predictable, probability of various events can be predicted. The application is clear. There are multiple dimensions of our communities that have the potential for significant events. Many are predictable, provable, and foreseeable. Why not insist on planning that identifies critical issues that might have serious consequences for the community? The engineering analogy must transfer to all aspects of government.

For different purposes and with different outcomes in mind, the same level of review, analysis, and planning must be undertaken by police, fire, public health, social services, facilities, public works, utilities, etc. Every public agency must invest in greater understanding of predictability and probability. Identified issues must be evaluated for impact, goals established and innovative strategies employed. Value can no longer be measured only by community wants and needs. In today's challenging world, the most precious ingredient may be a measure of predictable impact and how significant events and their costs can be avoided.

Chapter 3

Unforeseen Events – The Black Swans

Predictability is based on some indication or intuition that an event is bound to occur. Public leaders must consider a broad array of possibilities along with the potential for specific events to occur, the probability of the occurrence and its projected impact. In my view, the most critical question is, so what? If there is no impact, how important can it be? An event might be interesting but hardly consequential. We will return to this question in Part Three as we begin designing strategic plans, but it is still a centerpiece question that every manager and leader must employ.

This chapter introduces the highly improbable event...those that are unforeseen, unconsidered, and truly off the radar. The term 'Black Swan' used in this context was first used by Nassim Nicholas Taleb in his highly acclaimed book *The Black Swan—The Impact of the Highly Improbable* (Random House 2007.) The title was taken from the belief that, until black swans were seen in Australia, swans were always white. This totally changed the definition of a swan, which prior to that time had white coloration as a primary characteristic. Using this description, any true 'outlier' can now be considered a Black Swan.

High-consequence, unforeseen events have the greatest potential to positively or negatively impact the community and are capable of posing a threat to an entire state or country. They are often the transformative events that change the course of human history. Although at some level various outcomes may have been purposely sought, actual unanticipated results produced unplanned occurrences that altered entire societies. The discovery of Penicillin was an unplanned event, yet it transformed medicine and the treatment of infection. Most know the story. Alexander Fleming, a Scottish biologist and pharmacologist, had been investigating the properties of staphylococci in his laboratory, attempting to understand how it affected wound infection and septicemia. After returning to his laboratory from vacation on September 3, 1928, he found that a mold had formed in Petri dishes where he had been growing staphylococci. He noted that areas around the mold were clear of the staph organism but where it was not present the bacteria grew unabated. The mold, a common strain of the genus *Penicillium*, seemed to kill all staph colonies adjacent to it. After much experimentation, Fleming released his findings in 1929 and every reader knows the rest of the story. Penicillin became the most influential antibiotic in history and has saved countless lives since being fully developed and released as an antibacterial agent in 1940. For his discovery Fleming won the Nobel Prize and, in 1999, Time Magazine named him one of the 100 Most Important People of the Twentieth Century. This is not only a remarkable story, it is a wonderful example of a Black Swan-type of unanticipated event that changed human history. While researchers were constantly seeking answers to disease and infection, the actual discovery was purely by accident and the impact was beyond the wildest dreams of researchers.

Computers, the Internet, television, atomic energy and many other inventions were sought but had unforeseen consequences and applications. Steve Jobs and Steve Wozniak might have had a vision with no specific plan for it to totally transform society. But it did.

One does not have to conjure visions of a fairly large meteor striking the heart of downtown to invest in a discussion about totally unforeseen events that could wreak havoc. Science fiction has brought interesting visions of 'end of life' meteors advancing on Earth, or the aftermath of such events as mankind struggles to survive. Recent movies have portrayed a new ice age covering everything above 40 degrees latitude with a new glacier during a turbulent eight weeks after the oceans finally reached the warmth tipping point and the Atlantic conveyor screeched to a halt. All fun aside, significant historic trends are often ignited by unplanned and unforeseen events. As noted at the beginning of this chapter, there are 'unknown unknowns' that just can't be predicted or even foreseen. H.G. Wells conceived remarkable worlds and inventions, many of which have come true. But he did not attempt to predict social, cultural or economic outcomes derived from his interpretations. Generally, he focused on the adventure and left discussions of reality to his contemporaries and successors.

Let us conclude this point by saying that, as much as human beings want to predict the future, there are many variables that are outside our comprehension. Those we can conceive have too many contributing factors to ever allow practical review and prediction. I believe that many events can be identified and analyzed to the point that they can be partially predicted. Our role as public managers and leaders is to focus on those. True unknowns are outliers that cannot generally be factored into planning.

Partial Predictability

Based on good science and history, we can assume with some conviction that the wind will blow, the mountains will have snow during the winter, and it will be cold from November to March or April in the northern states. Experience allows us to make these 'predictions.' However, we do not know how hard the wind will blow, how much snow will fall and exactly where, or how cold it will be for how long. We know when hurricane season generally begins and ends but we cannot know how many storms will develop, how powerful they will become, if they will reach land and if so, where. In the geographic diagonal 'alley' from north Texas through Oklahoma, Kansas, Missouri, Nebraska, and Iowa, we know that weather patterns typically create tornados. But we cannot possibly know when or where they will form, how potent they will be, and where they might touch down. From a predictive standpoint, we can assume there will be some tornados this year. Unfortunately, we cannot possibly predict with any assurance how powerful they will be or what communities might be affected.

I term this 'partial predictability' because we have enough information to make predictions and even calculate probability to a certain extent, but can go no further. After that point, we enter the realm of impact moderation—attempting to prepare for an event that has some random potential of occurring. But if it does, it could be catastrophic. We don't *know* there will be a major earthquake in San Francisco in the next 500 years. But we *do know* that the city sits on a highly dynamic tectonic plate fault line that is building pressures that will at some point release enormous energy. We also *know* the wind will blow in Oklahoma and it will snow in Minnesota; we just don't know how much and what consequences will accrue.

Similar conditions exist for disease, road deterioration, crime, fires, medical emergencies, underground pipe failures, and hundreds of other situational forces that converge on communities. Unfortunately, we also know medical emergencies and crime will occur. We don't know where, how much or what kind. We can only prepare for eventualities. Public works engineers can identify sections of old water or sewer systems that have passed their predicted material life cycles and have increasing probability of failure. Due to so many variables (soil type, pipe quality and weather, for example), they don't know exactly where the system might fail, how large the break will be, or when it will occur (typically during rush hour!). But engineers can *partially predict* that it will indeed occur within a general time period and be prepared to moderate its impact on the community.

The winter of 2010 produced enormous amounts of snow in parts of the Northeastern U.S. Many communities were unable to contend with the amount of snow due to insufficient snow removal equipment, creating a great deal of public (and political) outcry. While snow is common in the winter, should those communities have purchased and had available twice as many snow plows and sanding trucks? This might have doubled capital costs and added significantly to operating and maintenance costs just to be prepared *in case* there was that much snow, which there had not been for decades. Did public administrators know it was going to snow? Certainly. But they had no way of knowing the amount of snow, number of storms, or timing of each separate event. In my view, they were prepared to the extent they could be as good managers. Additional expenditures to accommodate the potential of a '100-year' winter event would have been unwise. In this case, as with so many situations in public management, they were 'damned if they do, damned if they don't.' They would have been pilloried for being over prepared and wasting tax money if they had purchased the additional equipment and had ample personnel in place, just in case. The plight of many elected officials and public managers is that they are often placed in un-winnable situations when partially predictable major events occur.

Optimize vs. Maximize

The snowfall scenario indicates a conundrum for community leaders and public managers. Some communities gravitate toward optimization. That is, they want the 'Premium' version of a specific service. Some would purchase an over-abundance of snow removal equipment just to be prepared in the event there was an epic snowfall. Of course, for 9 out of 10 years, much of this equipment sits idle. Twenty-five years could elapse before snowfall warrants the expenditure. By then, the equipment may be outdated and even dysfunctional. Or, if it has been well maintained, imagine annual maintenance costs. It would have cost as much to maintain the equipment as to purchase it or to contract for additional private services during the big storm.

One city lamented to me that they would have to reduce the amount of street sweeping due to tight budgets. I assumed that they conducted street sweeping once or twice a month in the downtown core and was curious regarding how often they would now sweep streets. Their reply took me by surprise. They were contemplating reducing sweeping operations to only three days *per week*. I asked how often they currently swept downtown streets and was told it was done seven days per week! Most similarly sized cities sweep downtown streets from once per week to once per month. Talk about optimization! To be sure this is a great city with a lot of pride and the mayor wanted impeccable streets. At issue was the operation's growing cost.

This raises the question of how to *maximize capacity and capability* while optimizing available dollars. Returning to snow removal challenges in New England during the 2010 winter, cities with preexisting contingency contracts with private service providers and with sister cities were able to respond much better because they had maximized their existing fleet of snow removal and sanding vehicles by careful scheduling and during the storm had collaborated with surrounding municipalities. While they had chosen to avoid the 'premier' level of equipment, they maximized what they had by teaming with other cities. The outcomes were evident in media reports that applauded rapid responders and castigated those who were underprepared. Even though premium operations were able to respond quite capably, attention will soon return to the cost associated with maintaining the optimum fleet.

Corollaries exist throughout public agencies. Some cities and counties maintain very large law enforcement organizations, justified not by crime rates but by the prevention of crime. Or, public works replaces a large amount of water and wastewater infrastructure annually to reduce the probability of a major break. This is a local decision that involves questions surrounding the value of preemption.

The message is clear. For those circumstances or events that can be generally predicted, government leaders can prepare, at least to some extent. Preemptive actions can be budgeted and used to reduce probability and impact. Again using the utility example, properly scheduled preventive maintenance and replacement will reduce the probability of a utility system failure and can avoid serious impact to the community. Because there is an understanding that some forces are discernable and events predictable, every government agency must take time to identify potential events that pose a threat to the community. Issue analysis may indicate a practical need for more social service personnel to assist the homeless, more fire stations, more community patrol officers, a more responsive EMS system, or more water system testing. Analysis can help identify predictability and potential impact and is a precursor to remediation strategies employed to moderate impact. The events will occur. Consider these questions: 'Will the community be prepared?' and, 'To what extent should it be prepared?'

The challenge is to calculate associated cost vs. presumed value of preventing something that might occur in the future. This argument will continue to rage, especially in times of stressed budgets. How much money does government allocate to preventive or preemptive activities? My encouragement when doing community assessments is to weigh calculated impact *if* the event occurs against the cost of prevention or for offering a preemptive service. Leaders must invest in collaborative reviews that calculate partially or fully predictable events and what might moderate their impact. This takes foresight plus the ability and inclination to balance current needs with future possibilities. This will not get any easier in the years to come.

Predictable Surprise

There have been various ways of stating the phenomenon that becomes apparent when a shocking or significant event occurs after many warning signs that should have moved a community to action. Instead, there is a tendency to study things to death, become trapped in political gridlock, allow scientists to argue the point into obscurity, or just avoid it until it is too late. After the event, we shamefully acknowledge that we did indeed have data that allowed reasonable predictability and preparation. Building on fault lines is a classic example. We *know* the tectonic plates are moving; we know how fast; and we know what happens every so often when they reach a pressure 'tipping point'—they create earthquakes. It should be no surprise that an earthquake will occur in San Francisco or Seattle. Sooner or later, the catastrophic Big One will occur and of course, people will be 'surprised' when it does.

Another example of predictable surprise could have national or even global impact. A hundred years ago, science was incapable of explaining various natural phenomena. If natural events occurred and created unpredictable transformational periods, they were true Black Swans. Changing weather patterns that caused broad regional drought and subsequent crop failure were at that point Black Swan events because they were not understood and had insufficient scientific underpinning to offer much predictability. When they happened, they just happened and society did its best to recover. Unfortunately, throughout history entire societies have died and empires collapsed as a result of such events. As more information generates discussions about what event may occur and its probable impact, this very predictability has led to the phenomenon of *predictable surprise*. One potential catastrophic impact that we did not know about a hundred years ago but do now relates to the collapse of honey bee colonies across the nation.

As of 2010, three years after beekeepers started noticing sudden massive reductions of hive populations, biologists have neither determined the cause nor posed a remedy. This condition, which was first reported in 2006, is termed colony collapse disorder (CCD), and has the potential to hugely affect fully one-third of the food crops that rely on insect pollination. If this occurred a hundred years ago and the situation worsened until entire crops were decimated, it would have been a totally unpredictable Black Swan event. Now, however, it is a known situation that has a scientific basis. If it becomes a full-blown catastrophe, how many will be surprised? Certainly not farmers or entomologists!

Recent surveys suggest that hive losses have stabilized at approximately 30% annually but in many areas the fear is that hive losses will climb much higher. Should this occur, the impact on crop production could be enormous. This is no longer a Black Swan event because it is known, predictable and has probability associated with what happens *if*.

Though beekeepers, entomologists, and farmers are working diligently to solve the riddle of dying hives, if the massive die-off continues and crops are decimated, I guarantee that many, many people will be highly surprised that prices for many foods will skyrocket. Much like gasoline prices, as commodities become scarce, prices will escalate. Here's a tip: fund more research on what is destroying honeybees. If decision-makers choose to put money toward other priorities, they should not be surprised if serious consequences occur. It is a classic If-Then scenario.

My encouragement when doing community assessments is to weigh calculated impact if the event occurs against the cost of prevention or for offering a preemptive service. Leaders must facilitate collaborative reviews that calculate the probability of partially or fully predictable events and have the courage to invest in actions that might moderate their impact.

The Search for Certainty

It is human nature to seek stability and certainty. During the 1980s, The Futures Corporation conducted research to identify what motivated employees and citizens to collaborate, support or participate. At the time, I was interested in why people gravitated to or away from some managers and what factors drew people to some individuals and not to others. Ultimately, we isolated four factors:

Clarity – Regardless the level of trauma or situational difficulty, employees will gravitate to those who provide clarity. People want to know the facts, not a bunch of hooey.

Direction – A corollary of Clarity, people gravitate to those who provide direction. They plan, have a vision, and can point to a reasonable path forward. We often hear from citizens and employees, 'We just want clear direction...'

Truth – While there is certainly some aspect of ignorance in any group, when it comes down to crunch time, virtually everyone wants to know the truth...the unvarnished facts. This has been a debated subject for years. Many politicians will argue that citizens can't handle the truth or that they really don't want to know the truth. This is not the case. If you examine your own feelings, you will find that when the chips are down and it is decision time, you want to know the truth. Taking time to explain key issues and sharing potential impacts for each will pay huge dividends.

A dignified, harmonious and open style – Overall, people choose to follow those with warmth, grace, good nature, and a dignified style. This is one of the key attractors we use when discussing public leadership.

Now, you may ask what this has to do with the search for certainty. Very simply, the first three characteristics listed above are closely related to the human need for certainty. Whether employees or citizens, individuals and groups always desire clarity and direction, and demand truth. This is a major factor in people disconnecting from the political process - the truth is not always told and many facts are not revealed (or worse, distorted.)

As public leaders and managers, it is important to accept that your employees and community stakeholders will gravitate to the above factors because human beings pursue stability, which requires certainty. That is why unforeseen events are always dissected and related to past history in order to give context. We like to believe that we, in some way, knew an event was going to occur when we actually had no way of knowing.

Volatility and Instability

Two societal characteristics will become more prevalent in coming years. The world will face **more ambiguity** than ever before. What does this mean to our communities and leadership? Along with an escalating hunger for clarity and security, we will face a greater number of conflicting opportunities, needs, demands, and threats. The sheer number of variables is increasing exponentially. This phenomenon can be calculated through simple data analysis and be felt intuitively in every community.

What does this mean for public leaders and strategic thinkers? Due to the Internet and the enormous intrusion of public media into our lives, people are now more aware than at any time in history. As awareness grows, expectations grow, but fear and apprehension do as well. This has given rise to the second social characteristic that people are seeking— **stability**. During the period 1990 through around 2005, early and mid-career workers had a tendency to follow opportunity and money. Times were good and opportunity was abundant. There was a feeding frenzy of jobs, salaries, and benefits. This is no longer the case. Social scientists and more prescient economists predicted that this phase would end and it did. Today, the predominant need being expressed among working people in virtually every community is the desire for stability.

For planners, managers and elected officials, this has great value. For many years to come, perhaps the remainder of this century, there will be a preference for stability. This will be accompanied by the desire for clarity, direction and truth. Strategic plans must therefore address major issues and challenges and clearly express impact. People want to know the truth. Those who believe that most people would rather remain ignorant will be rudely awakened to this evolving social attribute. Even though it is discussed later, I encourage you to gather factual data, analyze it for predicted impact, and share it openly with the community. Then ask citizens, "Given the facts and circumstances, what do you prefer?"

The Illusion of Understanding

An element related to the discussion above is that people tend to create an illusion that they truly understand a phenomenon or event when, in fact, there is absolutely no grasp of what occurred and why. For partially predictable events, we know some of the factors and forces that are in play and that, given certain circumstances, a major event will (not may) occur. Again take tornados, earthquakes, hurricanes, epidemics, fires, water system failures, etc. We have the data. We understand the potential and why the event is probable.

But for totally unforeseen events, the Black Swans, there is a tendency to explore, analyze, and poke at them until we create an understanding of why they occurred. One can say that the advent of penicillin was just a matter of time. Or air travel, television, computers and the Internet were all certain to occur given the level of creativity available. But none of these major events could have been fully defined prior to their occurrence. While there were those who predicted aircraft and man's ability to achieve flight, travel to the moon or explore the oceans in submarines (Jules Verne wrote about air, space and underwater travel in the late 1800s) many believed those predictions were utterly mad. We tend to return to early musings to gain the illusion that various events or developments were a predetermined factor in the progress equation. In my view, this is perfectly fine. Why should we care if we believe today that there was a predictable pattern of development? Black Swan theorist Taleb feels this is a human weakness that leads to errant focus on events that cannot possibly be predicted. I don't see this as a weakness but as an attempt to comprehend.

The only danger for public managers lies in either *not* investing the time to think about the future or thinking and preparing *too much*. As noted earlier, this is a precarious Catch-22.

Avoiding the Big Whoops!

Every reader knows about the tremendous growth in the Southwestern U. S. Cities in Arizona, Nevada, New Mexico, and Southern California have attracted millions of people over the past 40 years. City planners and zoning commissions have struggled to accommodate the rush of new construction but communities have enjoyed great prosperity as populations expanded and businesses relocated to open-armed chambers of commerce, city councils and warm climates.

There is one slight issue: water. Research is now generally conclusive that annual precipitation in that geographic area has been unusually high for about 100 to 150 years, and many years during that time have been considered drought years. Unfortunately, the region appears to be returning to historic norms, which over the past thousand years have been approximately 40% less than this recent period. This is not to say that there cannot be years with high rain and snowfall, but overall the trend seems to be downward. And, as a side note, the most recent full decade (2000–2009) is now officially the earth's warmest decade on record, and 2009 tied with five other years as the second warmest year on record.

In addition, rationalists and naysayers are quick to discount historic data due to occasional precipitation surges. The winter of 2009–2010 was a good year for both snow and rainfall, allowing streams and reservoirs to regain much of their lost volume after several years of reduced precipitation. The Pacific jet stream created a classic El Nino weather pattern, bringing heavy rain and snow to Arizona and New Mexico, allowing a reduction of drought conditions. While this respite was welcome, it does not signal an end to drought issues.

Recently recharged reservoirs and underground aquifers can provide water for some time, but fossil (non-recharging) aquifers will soon be depleted. Without sufficient rain and snowfall over a period of years, recharging aquifers will not recharge fast enough to accommodate demand. If the data is even remotely accurate, what will the consequences be for the communities and people in this large area of the United States? Without adequate water the alluring qualities of sunshine and annual warm weather will be much less magnetic. The potential for escalating out-migration of both businesses and taxpayers is quite possible and certainly, expansion will be curtailed. Economic development will be inhibited and overall quality of life may suffer. This may seem a stark and rather gloomy assessment and some may question the data. But what if it proves to be accurate? Clearly, it means that we made a very sizeable miscalculation that could have very serious consequences.

Community leaders and elected officials cannot afford to ignore available data and must plan for the worst-case scenario. I suggest planning for various eventualities, but *all* stakeholders must have the opportunity to consider the data and its ramifications. One cannot blithely say, **Whoops!** and expect the community and deeply invested local business leaders to forgive and forget. When it comes to personal livelihood and business survival, a lot of negative energy can be generated in a short time.

Look at the data, consider various scenarios, and proceed with clarity, direction and as many facts as you can muster. If you understand social dynamics, you will understand that those who openly share information are typically accepted as leaders.

Risk and Public Leadership

I have lost count of the number of elected officials who have told me that, had they known the full extent of the difficulties and complexities inherent in managing state and local government, they would not have run for election. The same has been said by those who have joined government after working in the private sector. Those who have not worked for some time in government have no idea how much there is to know, how complex it is, and how many demands are placed on public leaders, administrators and employees. Indeed, public service is not for the timid.

In programs throughout the country, in my blog *Public Futures*, and in various writings, I encourage community leaders and public employees to err on the side of disclosure. Citizens have a right to know the extent of issues and challenges. They pay taxes that support programs and services and their awareness and understanding is crucial to gaining their support. Predictable and quasi-predictable events distill down into If-Then scenarios: *If* this occurs, *then* this will be the probable impact. If we take these preventive actions, we will: 1) avoid the event; 2) delay its occurrence; or 3) moderate its impact.

Public administrators and elected officials are central to every equation related to the provision of general operating services and to understanding and preventing potential harm to the community. They therefore must understand and accept a unique aspect of risk assessment. One of the most troubling aspects of risk deals with the personal risk associated with both identifying major potential events and preparing for them. My feeling is, if you are in a position of leadership, go ahead and take the point—walk out front. You are in a precarious position either way, but greater strength comes from a leading position than from an avoidance or deflective position. Gather the data, check its veracity and share it with others in the community. There is greater risk in not taking this approach than in taking the lead. If there is danger that the dam will break in specific circumstances, a true leader will know the facts, understand the consequences, openly share the information and facilitate dialogue about strategic approaches to avoid or delay the event or reduce its impact. You don't want someone to ask after a catastrophic event, Didn't you know this might happen? Didn't anyone warn you? "Well, er, yes, I think I might have heard something" just won't do.

The other facet of risk is really a corollary of the first. I meet many managers who take only 'good news' to elected officials. Or, they exclude harsh reality from plans and reports because elected officials accuse them of grandstanding to gain a greater share of the budget and might say that the numbers don't reflect a truth the public is willing to hear. I am a hard liner. Professional public mangers know their stuff and, if they conduct accurate analysis and make valid conclusions that reflect harsh reality, they must then take this to elected officials and they must listen. Many are unwilling to 'risk' sharing bad news and, if they do, it is true that many officials are not in an ideal position to react. Others refuse to listen.

I was once told by a state senator that, while I had good credentials and my numbers looked pretty good, he did not trust me because, "You feed at the public trough." Talk about angry! Before excusing myself, I told this man that I was a reasonably well-educated and dedicated public servant who worked 60-hour weeks and was paid to do the right thing. I explained that the analysis was accurate and had been reviewed by several local Fortune 500 corporations. My proposal, which would have saved state government close to $1 million annually with zero new funds

(I was seeking a change in language to give more latitude in how allocated funds could be spent), was defeated by a 12–8 margin.

The point here is that I could have not taken this proposal and the associated facts to the legislature to avoid the prospect of this reaction and to avoid being 'out front.' However, it was my job and the analysis was dead-on accurate. Now, many years later, I work with some managers who hesitate sharing overwhelming infrastructure, crime, health, socio-cultural, corrections, and other data, not because it is invalid, but because it presents a bleak picture to mayors, commissions, councils, governors and legislatures. And, it seemingly puts them in harm's way by being out front with tough but serious information.

I realize this is not a book on public leadership. That is *Leaving a Legacy*, which addresses a variety of leadership challenges. But please realize, there are many difficulties ahead and we must prepare. Elected officials need to know the truth. Conversely, they need to actively seek the truth and listen to experts who live their work every day. There is nothing worse than preventable disasters like the after-effects of Hurricane Katrina on New Orleans. Over the years, more than one warning was given. From subsequent reports, it appears that some of those who shared facts and raised warnings were chastised. The outcome was unacceptable, to say the least.

Look at the data, consider various scenarios, and proceed with clarity, direction and as many facts as you can muster. If you understand social dynamics, you will understand that those who openly share information are typically accepted as leaders.

Being Prepared for Challenge

The title of this series of books was taken from The Futures Corporation's original mission statement. The premise behind the statement is based on several fundamental questions: Are you prepared for the challenges ahead? Is your community or agency fully prepared or at least prepared to the extent it can be within budget parameters, levels of expertise, and preexisting variables (such as sitting on an active fault line)? Are you ready for predictable and unpredictable events? How do you know?

As you consider the possibility that perhaps you are indeed a futurist and a capable strategic thinker, there is no greater contribution than helping your division, department, community or state be fully prepared for the many challenges ahead. You are the current caretakers. You are at the helm. It is your turn to make the decisions and to create the path forward. There are no more potent questions than those pertaining to future readiness. With the number of currently known challenges and the unknown (but suspected) number of unknown events that could converge on your organization, community or state, there must be a greater sense of urgency.

As you begin Part Two, keep in mind the discussions, concepts and questions raised in Part One. Conceptual commonalities exist between predictability, probability, and totally unforeseen events. How you think about those will prove quite helpful as you begin grappling with a strategic thinking process that is specific to the management of government, developing communities and revitalizing community organizations.

For many years to come, perhaps the remainder of this century, there will be a preference for stability. This will be accompanied by the desire for clarity, direction and truth.

Part Two

Strategic Thinking & Planning:
A New Perspective for Elected Officials, Public Managers and Community Leaders

Part I introduced a variety of interesting thought processes related to studies of randomness, chaos, predictability, probability and preparing for future challenges. To a futurist or planning practitioner, it is not as though there are totally different schools of thought as much as various perspectives regarding future possibilities. While the pure scientist might revel in studies of random action, unforeseen consequence and chaos, an elected official cannot afford to live in that world. Public managers provide the foundation for normalcy or at least its pursuit. They preserve the framing and structure of society. While it is important that they understand concepts associated with probability theory, their attention is more profitably directed toward identifying current and impending problems, establishing goals, and creating strategies that produce desired community outcomes.

Part II builds on what I hope is now a greater appreciation for the value of prediction as it applies to community planning. While there are those who will remain firm in their conviction that the future cannot be predicted, I remain just as firm in my belief that much of it can be predicted if one understands the nature of *what* is being considered and *why*. Questions of possibility and probability will remain important keystones for public planning. As indicated by several earlier examples, elected officials and public managers can always assess various possibilities through competent analysis and apply probability calculations to the vast majority. Once accomplished, what then?

Some of my most significant frustrations have roots in the 'here to there' conundrum. How do public managers manage their way through current challenges, ascertain future issues, and generate cogent plans to simultaneously address both? Another book in the *Prepared for Challenge*™ series tackles operations planning and suggests several approaches available to managers. But day-to-day operations planning and operations management are far different from strategic planning.

The following chapters will explore what makes public sector strategic planning so different from business planning and why it is so important.

They will present a concrete definition of strategic planning and examine differences between public and private sector planning. It has also become evident that more clarity is needed about the component parts of state, county and city government executive planning and why elected officials and administrators must incorporate all elements to achieve internal *and* external progress toward goals.

Many readers will begin this book with a wealth of planning experience. Others will have much less or may have participated in various exercises that were less than stellar. To encompass the experienced, interested, and curious, as well as early career practitioners, I have taken time to define strategic planning and differentiate it from operations planning. There is a lively discussion about the psychology of planning, inherent benefits of the planning process, and why so many employees and managers resist. I also take some time to suggest methods that tend to enlist managers, supervisors and employees in collaborative planning efforts.

Because this book is dedicated to strategic thinking about the future, it would appear logical that planning follows naturally. There is always a struggle to generate a focus on future challenges while preparing plans that first recognize critical issues, then pose sensible goals, objectives and strategies. In many city; county and state agencies, there is concern, even fear, about the future. There are too many negatives, too many 'converging variables' that are overwhelming the ability of most agencies to meet demand, and both the level and intensity of that demand is increasing. My advice is to learn how to think about the future in constructive ways. It will be there; challenges are evident; and we have the tools, will, and experience to address most of them. All we need is deeper understanding and a strategic path forward.

A strategic planning *process* is much more important than the *product* it produces. Learning how to identify and articulate issues, then establish accurate goals, measurable objectives and strategies/actions that will drive budget allocation are skills every public administrator at every level should have. If this were the case, government would be much more effective, efficient, accountable and better prepared for the challenges ahead.

Chapter 4

The Rationale for Executive and Strategic Planning

Nothing can make the eyes glaze over faster than an announcement that the organization is preparing to undertake another strategic planning process. Throughout most organizations there will be lamentations and gnashing of teeth at the mere mention of an annual planning activity. "But we just did a plan in 2007, why do we have to do another plan so *soon?*" Or, "All we do is plan, plan, plan. The last four plans are sitting on the shelf, gathering dust. Why is *this* plan going to be any different?" And so it goes.

Has strategic planning become so laughable in public agencies? Top managers, executives and elected officials still seem convinced that planning has merit, and certainly, many professionals are exceptional planners. But quite apparently, the most common theme among employees is "Why do we have to do this? It's a waste of time."

As evidenced in Part I through various discussions about possible and probable futures, strategic thinking and planning have become the most critical elements of public management. Even though we have witnessed the advent of multiple planning activities over the past three decades, it is clear that overall strategic thought has become a key success factor that must be built into the fabric of every organization. In terms of professional development, the ability to think and plan strategically is one of the principal skills every responsible manager should possess and integrate into every work team, no matter how large or small. (Don't discount the previous statement. I have heard managers try to convince others that their department is just 'too large' or 'too small' to require strategic planning. Neither is accurate. Large and small organizations must engage in planning; it will benefit organizations of any size.) As noted throughout this book, it is important to understand that strategic planning is a *process* and not a program. While the central elements of a plan can be taught, it is the *process* of collaboratively planning and implementing that pays the greatest dividends.

The Concept of Executive Planning

It dawned on me one day that, from the early 1970s through the first decade of this new millennium—over the 35 years I have worked in and for state and local government—I have never seen or even heard of a comprehensive executive planning system, especially one formulated for government. Having done planning for Fortune 500 companies and many smaller firms with revenues ranging from $1 million to over $3 billion, as well as for state and local government, I am aware of and have been schooled in many planning approaches, often finding them merely retreads of previous processes. I would imagine that many readers have enjoyed using and incorporating various elements of Systems Theory, Malcolm Baldridge National Quality Award criteria, Balanced Scorecard, Six Sigma, Total Quality Management, Management by Objective, ISO 9000, its applications and updates (quality standards from the International Organization for Standardization in Geneva), and other continuous improvement approaches. Many senior managers have experimented with the older-style SWOT analysis (Strengths, Weaknesses, Opportunities, and Threats), as well as PEST reviews (Political, Economic, Social, and Technological), STEER analysis (Socio-cultural, Technological, Economic, Ecological, and Regulatory), and MBO (Management by Objective). All have merit if applied properly, but do they equate to a complete executive planning system for government? Not really. While various components have value, when used individually they don't connect all the dots.

Many state and local agencies have annual plans (some strategic, some not), operations plans, and annual budgets; communities are responsible for developing multi-year comprehensive plans; utilities are required to have solid waste, water and wastewater system plans; and public safety agencies have annual plans that detail disaster response, crime prevention and homeland security measures. Even with this volume of planning activity, I have only occasionally seen a local government that has an aligned planning system with guidelines, internal training, linkages, templates, shared measurement, and a summarized annual reporting process. Though I am somewhat biased, the city of Henderson, Nevada has one of the best integrated strategic and financial planning systems I have seen. The bias is due to Henderson using the strategic planning system first created by The Futures Corporation. I must say, however, the city has taken it to a remarkable level. Under the guidance of Michael Cathcart, strategic planning in Henderson is imbedded in the budget office and fully integrated into annual performance and financial planning. Programs and services have established goals, measurable objectives and specific actions for which funds are allocated. While many local governments have some elements of strategic planning and performance budgeting processes, most do not have fully integrated systems. And, as we'll learn later, few have stated program objectives that are truly measurable.

In my view, the absence of any such comprehensive planning system is one of the multiple factors that inhibit the progress, adaptability and stability of state and local government. This is especially critical now in an era of declining revenues, greater public scrutiny and the importance of transforming to leaner, more accountable government.

It would seem apparent that for practical reasons and to promote efficiency, it is essential to pursue more integrated planning at the executive level of state and local government. That typically means involvement by all executive department directors as well as by commissioners, city managers and mayors who serve as chief executive officers (it is not as critical for governors to be deeply involved). Generally, elected officials receive plans but are not instrumental in their development. To properly plan, develop, and operate essential community services, local governments need an overall executive planning process that includes strategic planning, operations planning, organization improvement planning, and financial planning.

Even though public planning has evolved considerably over the past decade, those efforts will continue to be driven and defined by four factors:

1. The importance of understanding current and emerging issues and preparing for future challenges that have high probability of significant community impact.

2. Greater attention dedicated to accountability through efforts that assess program value and contribution to the community, and the explicit requirement that every program show measured performance, progress toward planned outcomes, and value for resources expended.

3. Greater clarity about agency and program missions (why they exist), long-term goals (expected outcomes), annual objectives, tangible performance indicators and scheduled strategies/actions that will be undertaken to achieve goals and objectives.

4. Detailed reports that describe agency and program efforts toward continuous internal improvement. Regardless of funding levels, the question must be posed: How is this agency improving its efficiency, effectiveness, productivity, and quality while keeping costs as low as possible?

The basic question is, 'What does Executive Planning for city, county and state government entail?' I recommend that every governor, mayor, city manager, municipal board, county commission, etc. establish a series of plans and reports that address specific aspects of public management. Four annual documents should be required from all agencies:

Strategic Plan – Strategic in nature and addresses *only* the major issues and challenges the agency (and ultimately the state, county or community) is facing, along with goals, objectives, strategies and actions. It is *issue-driven* and pertains to existing or predicted problems encountered by agencies responsible for dealing with them. Some issues will be shared among multiple agencies but application of strategies (how issues are addressed) will differ.

Operations Plan or Summary – Defining for each department and its component parts the various missions, operating (as opposed to strategic) goals, planned annual outputs and expected outcomes for *general operations.* Hard performance metrics are included for each output and clear outcomes are stated. This plan answers the question, 'What are you doing and what is the community or taxpayer getting for the dollars spent?' It is typically a mission-driven summary document that describes the various operating elements of each department along with a description of what is being provided for an annual budget established to maintain current operations.

Internal Improvement Plan – A concise report that describes internal issues or circumstances that inhibit the agency from achieving its mission then proposes remedies and provides an estimated cost if new money is required. Once identified, most internal issues are addressed with already appropriated and allocated funds. They are merely re-allocated to address specific high-priority internal issues. This simple report generates significant management commitment to continuous improvement and demonstrates to executives that each agency is invested in reviewing and addressing problems that impact the quality or efficiency of internal operations. Its inherent value is that it formalizes internal improvement through a process that offers great latitude but still focuses resources on agency development. Even though they are highly sought, you do not need to win a Baldridge Award to have great continuous improvement processes!

Annual Report – A composite report that summarizes the major elements of Strategic, Operations, and Improvement plans. These have many formats; some are quite extensive, others are summaries. But all provide the chief executive, board, council, commission, and public with an overview of what each agency is facing, its general operations, how it is improving, and what it is accomplishing for the funds expended.

I can hear what some readers are thinking: 'That is too much! We don't have time for all those plans and reports!' Here's the interesting thing. After working with many state agencies, cities and counties over the years, most already have a variety of required plans and reports. Rarely, however, do I find a comprehensive executive planning approach that even partially connects key planning efforts to a central process. Some get close but I have seen no single system (especially retread business systems that are being sold to government) that I would fully recommend. (If you have such an integrated system, I would love to see it!) Done well, it is much faster and efficient, generating less heartburn and providing better overall reporting. The genesis of the many forces contributing to the need for evolved planning systems matters little. What does matter is that the magnitude of restricted funds and growing needs now confronting state and local government demand greater commitment to comprehensive executive planning and resource allocation.

Strategic Planning vs. Operations Planning

There is apparently more confusion about the difference between strategic and operations plans than with any other plan types. Very simply, operations plans deal with day-to-day operations – getting the basic job done. They are not strategic and do not necessarily grapple with major strategic issues (although some operational issues can be quite significant and may be elevated to 'strategic' status). Strategic plans identify critical strategic issues and challenges that are now or may someday impact the community. Some are 'over the horizon' but need to be addressed preemptively. Others are based on the possibility and probability they will occur and will have significant impact. Still others are considered inevitable and need to be addressed to prepare the community for an anticipated outcome (like Baby Boomers accessing social and financial services in large numbers beginning in 2008 and multiplying between 2012 and 2018).

An operations plan is more tactical than strategic. It is more about *how* the work is done and *what* is accomplished for the allocated funds than about *why* the work is done or how it affects long-term community direction. On a week-to-week basis, managers are more interested in accomplishing work than they are in identifying and addressing critical issues and challenges connected to some potential future event or situation. As in business, 'operators' are the people who plan and execute day-to-day work activities. Even though we occasionally ask them to be strategic thinkers, their operations plans deal with the realities of accomplishing basic missions.

Although repeated several times in this book, it is essential that there is a general distinction for government that clarifies that strategic planning should address major issues and challenges that will or may affect a specific population or the entire community. Strategic plans are *issue-driven*. For the most part, they do *not* address day-to-day operational activities or departmental performance and do not explain what the public receives for their tax dollars. Conversely, operations plans are *mission*-driven. As described earlier, they review individual missions, explain services, clearly express key outputs, outline expected outcomes (contributions or achievements), and provide performance metrics that are an intrinsic component of performance budgets.

With a 'base' operations budget, most stakeholder questions seek insight regarding what is being done with budget dollars and what outputs are being delivered. A manager answers these questions by describing what activities (outputs) the department or division undertakes and what results (outcomes) it expects to achieve. Again, these are not strategic actions, but activities budgeted and scheduled to accomplish the organization's basic mission. The question is, 'What are you doing and accomplishing for the funds you were given?'

Unfortunately, of the many strategic plans we review every year, most are hybrids containing various characteristics of both operations and strategic plans with some aspects of annual reporting tossed in. Our research has shown that far too few public agencies take time to develop and maintain either strategic or operations plans. Quite often, there are no formal (or even informal) internal plans describing the activities of various departments, the programs and activities for which each is accountable, or the basic outcomes each is expected to produce. However, more progressive states, cities and counties require departments to have at least rudimentary operating plans that explain what services are offered to whom, what outputs are delivered, and how outcomes are measured. Critically, there are also few local governments that tie performance measures to budget allocation and create a "triage" system based on what services are most essential to sustain an economically vibrant, safe, and harmonious community. Instead, the annual budget appropriation and allocation process is too often a battle among departments that pitches director against director and occasionally elected officials against each other as they collectively grapple with service priorities.

Operations Plans vs. Business Plans

There seems to be a continuous attempt to introduce business planning into government. On the surface, this cyclic phenomenon always seems like a good idea to elected officials, who often come from private business. Unfortunately, it generally proves to be a waste of time that further drives employees away from any meaningful planning. Why is this?

There is an attraction to language that purports to deliver the same results in government as in business. Similar topics are found in business and operations plans but lead to different destinations. Both desire efficient and effective operations but one ultimately serves to generate market share and profit, the other provides services to the community. I recently read of a governor who was pushing all state agencies to develop 'business plans.' This is well-meant but misguided. Because his background includes senior-level employment in a multi-billion dollar company, it is the only context he can apply to state government. As with many governors, he has also appointed several former business executives to state director positions rather than seasoned, well-prepared public administrators who are subject matter experts. While those appointees may ultimately become effective public administrators, appointing them can prove to be a mistake because the learning curve is so steep that much of their time is spent trying to understand how government works. And, as in federal government, many will have short tenure and the process will soon be repeated with another appointment. In such situations, there is marginal lasting value.

If the governor and his executive team can be convinced to institute a public sector-centric executive planning process as introduced here, state agencies will be more capable of producing and sustaining desired results, regardless of who is at the helm. And, both seasoned public managers and appointees will more likely embrace the process.

As a final note, while there are some shared characteristics in business, strategic and operational planning, each process and plan exists for a different purpose. Once crafted, they provide the foundation for the third element of executive planning: overall improvement planning. Ultimately, planning seeks to improve external and internal conditions, address issues, and strengthen the community. Internally, it leads to greater efficiency, productivity, quality and managed costs. However, unless all elements of executive planning are incorporated, results will fall below expectations.

Chapter 5

What Exactly IS Strategic Planning?

Fundamentally, strategic planning provides the means to, A) identify internal and external problems B) establish long-term goals (outcomes) and shorter-term measurable objectives (outputs or outcomes); C) agree on sensible strategies, and D) develop actions that detail what steps will be taken to actualize strategies to achieve goals and objectives. These basic planning elements have been around for decades but are often confusing when various models mix applications from private to public organizations.

The art of planning reflects intent to calculate direction, purpose, and destination, then develop a reasonably efficient path to achieve progress. However, there is more to it. There is general clarity about the word 'strategy.' Webster defines it as, 'Skill in managing or planning, especially by using stratagems.' This feels a bit cumbersome. In my view, a strategy is:

> An activity that, when properly devised, calculated, and executed, will accomplish intended goals and objectives, which will in turn address identified issues and challenges. A strategy is a broad action. It is an *approach*, whereas an action is a specific activity that represents an element of the overall strategy and is a step toward goal completion.

Strategic planning is based on the premise that, once we have identified and analyzed important issues and challenges (i.e. problems) we can devise a variety of strategies and actions that will allow us to properly address them. A strategic plan for a public agency will therefore identify key issues and challenges, establish long-term goals and short-term (usually annual or biennial) objectives, and present strategies and actions that are calculated to provide solutions. A strategic thinker is constantly reviewing data to identify critical issues, analyze them, and then pose reasonable, cost-effective remedies. Strategic thinking allows us to produce the rationale for and content of practical strategic plans. Think: ISSUE >GOAL > OBJECTIVE > STRATEGY > ACTION > MEASUREMENT.

A problem arises when mixing too many applications into planning discussions. The military uses similar language but has a different context for mission, goal, strategy and action. Similarly, business uses identical words but applies the associated activities differently. A mission to build a viable, sustainable, and profitable business is far different from a mission to protect and serve the community. Public sector strategic planning has for too long been a hodge-podge of business and military planning language and approaches that have not morphed into a separate discipline for government agencies. This has led to confusion and misunderstanding about the nature of public sector strategic planning and why it is so important to efficient government.

Early in my career, I used various planning formats, some of which will be familiar to the reader. MBO (management by objective), POME, (problem, objective, method, evaluation), PERT (program evaluation and review technique), and others were all the rage in the 1970s and 1980s. Variations of Zero Base Budgeting were used to balance tight state and local government budgets and to ensure progressive, efficient program management. (Unfortunately, many variations led to budget reductions that were poorly calculated and resulted in serious harm to both agencies and citizens.) There is no shortage of formats to choose from. The secret is knowing which ones apply to public challenges and the unique characteristics of public agencies. I have found some value in various elements of virtually every planning format I have used. All have merit. The key is to understand government and where to apply the various pieces and parts of dozens of formats that have emerged over the years. That takes familiarity with public administration – something rarely gained without experience as a public manager.

Contributions from Business

Over the years, a variety of business writers have attempted to convert business planning to public terminology. As a leader in the Management by Objective movement, George Morrisey wrote *Management by Objectives and Results* (Addison-Wesley Publishing, 1970) and then attempted to convert many of the more salient principles for use in the public sector in *Management by Objectives and Results in the Public Sector* (Addison Wesley, 1976). I was an early adopter of MBO and believe its principles remain viable today. However, as a working public administrator, I found Morrisey's articulation of goals and objectives to be a poor fit for government agencies. As often emphasized in this book, goals and objectives are NOT activities. They are outcomes or valued, measured outputs. So, while many of the guidelines suggested by Morrisey remain valuable, examples for public agencies do not fit reality. For instance, examples such as 'To complete conversion of bureau records to microfiche by October' were provided as examples of 'objectives.' This is not, however, a viable objective…it is clearly an action. As we'll explore later in greater detail, the critical question is, 'What is gained by the completion of that action?' *That* is the objective.

Please don't misunderstand the comment above. I believe Morrisey is a true pioneer of strategic planning and embrace much of his philosophy. In many ways, his early work serves as a foundation for my current system, along with the work of Bill Smith of Motorola, who in 1986 first formulated the methodology for Six Sigma. In some form or another, the work of Deming, Juran, Taguchi and Senge have all contributed to various systems that advocate issue identification; clear, measurable goals and objectives; sensible strategies and actions; and an integrated process that imbeds continuous improvement and learning into the culture.

As noted previously, strategic thinking and planning is NOT a program. It is a *process* that must be learned, practiced and taught to others. While it looks generally the same and uses much of the same language in public and voluntary agencies, planning has a different overall approach in private business.

With emphasis, let me again say that strategic planning in government agencies must be *issue-driven*. In most cases, there would be no agency if there were not issues or problems that created community needs in the first place. Law enforcement is a perfect example. If there were no crime, traffic issues, or domestic disputes, there would be no need for police officers. The same is true with fire departments, public works departments, emergency medical services, health departments, social services, etc.

Every public agency serves a purpose designed, we assume, to serve a community need. If the need doesn't exist, the program is unnecessary. Even though some public employees recoil at the thought that their services might be unnecessary, most public programs have evolved to meet a need or address an issue. A strategic thinker must consider this fact as a detached clinician. Examine any facet of public service and seek to understand the genesis of that particular program and why it exists. The key issues that provided the impetus to develop or expand a program or agency generally become readily apparent.

Even those departments that provide central services, such as tax assessment and collection, development services, building inspection, election services, license renewal, or general administration cannot effectively plan unless they strive to address identified issues, challenges or needs. How else would process improvement occur? Even the most general administrative organization evolved to accomplish a required public service. And in every general administrative service there must be some intent to improve efficiency, responsiveness, productivity or quality. As reviewed earlier, it is important to remember that the general activities of an organization are not strategic—they are operational. In strategic planning, it is critical to understand the issues being addressed. For each issue, consider how you will *strategically improve that stated condition or problem.*

Strategic planning is an approach to problem identification and problem solving; it provides the means to address challenges and improve the agency, its programs, and the entire community. As applied to public agencies, my definition of strategic planning is:

A system of long-term thinking and planning that establishes rationale and criteria for program, department, and community improvement. It also provides the basis for performance-based budgets and evaluation systems that allow review of program and employee performance, service quality, and productivity.

Emphasis must be on developing a system for strategic thought that promotes the long view and broader horizons than addressed in operations planning. The ultimate goal is to improve the community, agency and program performance, preparation, and the ability to moderate or avoid major negative events. With that in mind, I encourage accurate metrics that promote outcome and output measurement while providing the basis for calculating overall progress toward goals. Were I an elected official, I would be asking, *'Are we improving* both *the organization and the community? How do we know?'*

Why Plan?

Why do we plan in the first place? Very simply, when all contributions are distilled down to a basic essence, it is to *improve*. It is also to maintain established standards that preserve a specified or desired level of quality. Even with such a variety of emerging variables, there are always opportunities to improve and this should be the central theme of all public planning activities.

Given the discussion in Part I, it would seem strange to not include a parallel planning rationale dedicated to preventing or moderating the impact of highly predictable events or situations. Even this perspective, however, assumes that one is *improving* the probability, number of options, or the capacity to moderate impact. Whether you are improving the chances for something to occur or not occur or, if it occurs, to reduce its potential to harm the community, your purpose is to improve the odds or outcome. Keep this in mind as you are developing issue statements and determining how to answer the question, *'So what?'*

The underlying premise of public sector strategic planning is that there is value associated with identifying important issues and challenges, then establishing long-term goals, annual objectives, and detailed actions/strategies. These actions/strategies not only address stated issues but also strive to improve performance, productivity, community and personal well-being. Planning activities must focus on the *most critical factors* impacting the state, local community or specific client base and seek the most effective and efficient means to address them. Though this sounds fairly simple, it is astounding how few agencies have thoughtful planning processes in place and how few have created an aligned, comprehensive planning environment.

For some, merely improving quality, operating efficiency or productivity does not provide sufficient rationale for establishing a strong planning system. While improvement is the central theme, I would suggest more reasons for strategic planning:

- It identifies critical issues and challenges an agency, the community or specific stakeholders are facing.

- A properly crafted plan allows the reader (or community) to understand the rationale behind various programs and associated budget requests. Requesting funds to maintain general operations does not always generate strong program or budget support.

- Accountability and transparency become foundational elements of programs due to clear goals, measurable objectives, strategies and actions that detail what is being done, why it is important, and how progress will be measured.

- Strong plans will generate stronger annual reports that 'showcase' what an agency or the government has undertaken and how these efforts have strengthened the community.

- There is a more direct and understandable strategic path to an established vision and better acceptance of government's role in achieving desired community outcomes.

Purists would argue that planning is undertaken mainly because it is a manager's responsibility. It is an element of expected administrative and elected official performance. Most management texts would support the assumption that, whether elected or appointed, public managers are expected to develop and follow sensible plans. While planning is at times resisted, exceptional planners provide more efficient, higher quality and more productive, accountable government.

Collaborative Outcomes

While recently working with a large public organization, one of the senior elected officials mentioned to me that economic and workload issues had noticeably reduced employee morale. Further, a variety of challenges seemed to have caused a significant number of employees to withdraw, 'lay low,' and not get involved with various activities. He asked if I thought the planning process might have a positive impact on frustrated employees.

My response was straightforward. Typically, planning produces a document that generates little notice and may have little direct impact on those who developed it. This is especially true if a plan is developed by a small group of senior managers who do not seek employee input. However, if planning proceeds as a *collaborative process* and involves a significant number of employees, and has community representation, it can have a lasting positive impact. I encouraged this official to develop an inclusive process—get people involved with data gathering, analysis, goal setting, action plans, and performance criteria. If employees help identify and analyze the issues and challenges facing the community, they are more likely to become energized, rally behind key issues and find new purpose in their work. As we'll explore later, *excluding* employees can turn a potentially vibrant, exciting process into a lifeless, dull exercise with little long-term value.

- A strong, durable foundation for management and leadership development;

- Constant promotion of thoughtful organizational change and a focus on the future;

- Clear, sensible quantification for reviewing potential events that may be predictable or preventable; and, for providing options for moderating consequences to the community.

With so much to gain, it seems curious that there is not more emphasis on reality-based strategic planning in public administration degree programs. What little planning instruction there is seems antiquated and not relevant to the challenges and needs of modern public agencies. Contribution engenders legacy. Being able to identify challenges, analyze their cause, develop prudent strategies and successfully implement them provides the type of continuous improvement and progress we expect from public organizations. It is unfortunate that so few people think in terms of a planning legacy.

Most managers and supervisors have historically been captivated by the operational aspect of their work and its focus on task completion. What about the final result? What will the ultimate contribution be? What impact will that manager have on the employees he or she supervises? Will they learn and grow? And will they become creative, insightful planners who can also analyze, strategize and implement quality programs? The planning process embodies more than the simple tasks of establishing a mission, creating a vision and agreeing on general agency or program goals. It is a process of investigation, learning, and implementing in a collaborative environment so the entire organization progresses and evolves.

Some time ago, I was contacted by a large county that wished to complete a strategic plan. Managers were interested in learning the system developed by The Futures Corporation, but there were many who exhibited a good measure of skepticism. The County Administrator told me bluntly, "We have spent a considerable amount of money on consultants over the past two years trying to complete a strategic plan. Our people are tired of meetings and are pretty confused about whether strategic planning is really worth the trouble."

Though on the surface this may almost appear humorous, it is a sad and accurate commentary on how many planning processes go awry. They are too complex, take too long and are not based on sound training that teaches the essence of *public sector* planning. And when all this work results in little or no measurable progress, participants are left more cynical and demoralized than when it all began.

With some facilitation, training, and an illuminated path forward, the county had a very potent plan completed in less than five months.

Chapter 7

The Psychology of Planning

There is an interesting psychology to planning that in many ways both guides and contaminates the process. Since we were children, we have been taught to be action-oriented. Virtually everyone has heard the words, 'Get off your rear and do something!' Or 'Don't bring me problems, bring me solutions!' Action has become a central characteristic of the American culture and pervades all levels of business and government. This is not a bad thing. In fact, it has been one of the driving forces behind our successful culture and way of life.

Each of us learns early in our careers that action is expected and that being busy is highly acceptable. Young employees are taught by word and deed that action plans and 'To Do' lists are a sure-fire way to become successful. But then these same individuals are asked to think strategically. They are asked to describe the most significant issues that their community, agency or work team faces and to list those goals and objectives that will guide the organization to higher levels of achievement. Many find this difficult because they have always been involved in day-to-day operations that focus on activity planning and have been conditioned for years by admonitions to 'do something.'

Activity Lists Are *Not* Plans

As implied in Chapter Four, over the years strategic planning has become skewed toward operations planning and many of the *strategic* plans I see are 15% strategic and 85% operations. Why is this important? Because strategic planning is a sequential process of thinking that is patterned after the scientific method. It is based on deductive reasoning and is a process that must be learned and applied to real situations. During planning exercises, I ask participants to review key community and organization issues. In virtually every situation, issues or problem statements are articulated as *solutions*, instead of true issue statements. Typical 'problem statements' might be, 'We need more computers;' 'We need more staff to get the job done;' 'The department needs more patrol cars to meet community policing needs;' 'We need to raise K–6 immunization levels.' And so forth. None describe the underlying problems.

Psychologically, most managers revert to old habits, developing plans that are aggregates of activity lists. Even though valuable, these actions are not properly stated goals or objectives and are detrimental to planning because they promote plans that are nothing but large 'to do' lists. I tell clients, 'It is great to bring me solutions, but first explain the problem and the ultimate outcome you would like to achieve.'

True to my redundant nature, the following discussion will be further developed in Parts III and IV when plan elements are thoroughly reviewed. However, it is important to achieve clarity about the natural tendency to gravitate to action statements instead of creating accurate issue statements, goals and objectives *prior* to listing strategies and actions.

Issues must be stated as a problem that relates to but is not driven by a) the organization's mission, or b) the organization's ability to fulfill its obligations within the context of its expertise. If the organization's mission deals with child health, then issues related to child health are addressed and should, to the extent possible, be stated in statistical terms in order to emphasize the true nature of the problems/issues. The issue is that 'Immunizations have dropped from a high of 88% in 2005 to less than 62% in 2010.' Or, 'During FY 2010, 346 children under the age of

12 were seriously injured in automobile accidents due to not wearing seatbelts.' Including potent data communicates the gravity of the situation.

The same would be true for agencies responsible for law enforcement, tax collection, infrastructure, utilities, fire protection, court administration, corrections, etc. Problem statements/issue categories would be in subjects related to those agency missions—in other words, what they are there to address. By communicating statistical data, the issue, or problem, is revealed and stated in clear, understandable terms. The *solution* will be stated later as one or more actions and strategies because it indicates *how* the program intends to achieve the objective.

As in writing issues as solutions, there is also the tendency to focus on solutions when writing goals and objectives. Though addressed more specifically later, it is worth mentioning that adults have a psychological tendency to write goals and objectives as action statements and *not* as true goals and objectives. Without exaggeration, I would say that 95% of all goals and objectives are written as actions and/or strategies. As explained previously, this is due to the almost innate tendency to focus on activities or solutions and not on ultimate outcomes or achievements related to an organizational mission.

A goal is *not* 'To outfit all patrol officers with new wireless remote laptops by July 2012' or 'To move toward a team-based workforce before the end of 2012.' The first is a specific action, the second a strategy. Neither is a *goal*. The point here is that people tend to think in action terms. This is not bad but can frustrate the effort to promote strategic thinking and create strategic plans. Understanding how people think is very important to your planning effort. Planning coordinators or consultants must realize that human nature plays a significant role in identifying, categorizing and articulating an organization's mission, vision, values, issues/challenges (threats), goals, objectives and actions/strategies. Knowing that people typically plan first in action terms rather than in outcome or achievement terms will help when deciphering initial work done by employees.

The secret is to understand basic human nature and that adults have been encouraged for decades to think in action terms. By learning about and understanding their own tendencies to write actions instead of goals and solutions rather than clear issue statements, employees will recognize how to convert solutions back into powerful issue statements and actions into potent goals and objectives. They will also be able to recognize the difference between action planning and strategic planning and how existing plans can easily be re-worked into viable strategic documents.

Chapter 8

Why Strategic Planning Fails

During many adventures assisting city, county and state agencies with strategic planning, I began to see a pattern that provides evidence as to why strategic planning fails. The common refrains include at least three pervasive themes: there is never enough time, plans are not seen as useful tools by managers, and planning interrupts essential operating activities.

These arguments carry some weight. In many state and municipal governments, the number of employees has declined as workload has increased, reducing the time available for collaborative planning. People are busy and essential duties have priority. However, if done properly, is planning really that intrusive?

Whenever possible, I refute with some vigor the position that public employees have unnecessarily proliferated during tough economic times, are somehow substandard performers, and are less capable than their private sector counterparts. In various articles and programs, I have expressed the view that population growth and public demand have combined to drive the need for more public services. This is not associated with a political party and there is no formula that automatically generates more government employees while private employers struggle to survive. More accurately, as society becomes more

Planning the FUTURE

complex, communities demand more services to accommodate a greater number of specialized needs. Constituencies grow and demand services through new programs.

As a whole, public employees produce more work and contribute more to their communities than they get credit for. Having worked for and around public agencies for many years, I can honestly say that skill, commitment, and grasp of issues tend to trump other factors that inhibit completion of high-quality strategic plans.

In addition to inhibiting factors related to time, frequency, or perceived value, there are several others that appear to be the most prominent reasons for outright failure or less than desirable outcomes.

Confusion About What vs. How – There is a bit of social psychology associated with understanding why there is a tendency for managers to focus more on conducting operations than on planning. As suggested in the previous chapter, from an early age we are taught to *do* something, to be active and 'do it now.' From a psychological standpoint, most adults gravitate to actions; they focus on *how* to do something rather than on first considering *what* is happening, *what* should be done and *why* it is important. Managers faced with many responsibilities and growing demands have little choice but to concentrate on the most essential activities that produce program results. Public sector strategic plans are based on critical issues and challenges. Identifying *What* the issues are and *Why* they are important is a strategic process. Addressing *How* those issues are resolved relates to some degree to *operations planning*. This can be confusing because this is where elements of strategic thinking converge with operations planning; to compound matters, there are elements of both in a properly developed strategic plan. Understanding how the elements differ is critical.

Too Much Top-Down Planning – All too often, elected officials or senior management teams launch into planning programs that involve only department or division managers and rarely involve other employees. Execution requires a feeling of ownership that is best gained through inclusion. From my experience, the employee base is critical to developing meaningful plan content because of the enormous amount of collective knowledge that resides with the people doing the work. Frankly, who knows the organization better, employees with 20+ years' experience or elected officials? I am not discounting the knowledge, skill or desire of elected officials. I am merely suggesting that tenured employees are subject matter experts who are typically much more aware of external and internal issues than elected officials and are often the best people to suggest solutions.

For example, I was doing some organization planning work for a city in Wyoming some years ago and asked that I be allowed to selectively visit with employees at all levels. The city manager agreed and was quite interested in hearing about my conversations and what information was shared. In a single conversation with front line public works employees, I was told about a broad array of issues with the city's sewer and water systems, which areas of the systems would fail and why, and how priority should be applied to both maintenance and repair. I asked if they had shared this information with senior managers and the reply was, 'They never ask us.' Tenure among this group averaged 22 years and their knowledge and skill level was exceptional. Subsequently, the city manager established planning teams comprised of employees from all levels of the city and captured an entirely new level of technical expertise. This saved time and money, but also created a more collaborative planning environment that is still paying dividends. Not every employee needs to be involved with planning—that would create a cumbersome process. But a good cross section is wise and produces many benefits.

Those doing the work on a daily basis must be involved with issue identification along with other elements of the planning effort. To the extent possible, involve as many employees as practical. Similarly, every departmental unit (division, section, or program) that has a specific purpose or mission should have its own plan. Planning must be guided from the top but be actively pursued at all levels. Senior managers set the tone, establish planning as a priority, provide proper training and launch the process but tactically engage a wide variety of employees and encourage planning throughout the organization.

Lack of Understanding About Planning – Even though many individuals have played a role in some form of public planning, very few people in state and local government have been professionally trained in the most fundamental elements of strategic thinking and planning. Many have participated in various planning exercises but few of those included high-quality training. To be successful there must be training and an orientation to planning and it must be part of a core development program for all employees. If there is properly conducted training on strategic plan development, within one or two 'employee generations' there will be a culture of planners who understand the language, process and value of continuous community and operations improvement through effective planning and implementation.

Unclear Missions – Every unit within a public agency must be able to clearly state its mission, yet many cannot do so. If a work team, bureau, section or division does not clearly understand its mission or why it exists, it will be challenged to sustain the desired level of progress, productivity or quality. In many organizations, I have found sections or work teams that have almost identical missions, often duplicating efforts with little or no collaboration. More disturbing are those organization elements that have no or unclear missions that employees can't articulate. I am not saying that every employee must be able to recite the mission. But I am saying that they need to know what the work unit, section, bureau or division is there to accomplish. If I was an elected official and a supervisor or division manager could not clearly explain the unit's mission, I would be concerned.

Too Many Planning Formats – In many municipal and state governments, there is no central planning format with which all employees are familiar. Some progressive municipal governments or independent departments have sought training in strategic planning, developed a sound format, and have installed it as a key element of the management culture. Unfortunately, this is the case in only a small number of the organizations I have visited over the years. In one state government, I found at least one hundred different planning formats among state agencies. When I met with the Division of Financial Management, which oversees strategic planning, I was told that they did not want to dictate a single format or standardize content. I asked if they allowed each state agency to do its budget in whatever format they chose. Of course they thought this was silly and proceeded to explain that there was a prescribed standardized budget format and all agencies had to comply. Is budgeting more important than plans that reveal major challenges, issues, goals, annual objectives, and agency action plans? Absolutely not. Strategic plans must drive budgets...budgets do *not* drive planning. Unfortunately, in that state this is not the case. No wonder people are confused. To be successful, there *must* be one planning format, standardized language, and performance expectations, similar to a commitment to one budget format that is understood and followed by all agencies within that state, city or county.

Goals and Objectives Are Poorly Stated – There is almost a total misconception as to what constitutes a goal or an objective. While this is another redundant theme, *out of all the plans reviewed each year, less than five percent have properly stated goals and objectives.* Virtually all are stated as actions or strategies—*not* as true goals or objectives. Even though mentioned earlier and covered more completely later in this book, let me be clear—a goal (long-term) or an objective (shorter-term) is a measured output or outcome; it is *not* an activity. Refurbishing a bridge, immunizing a population of school age children, training employees on a new software system—are all activities. The results or *outcomes* of these actions are the goals and objectives. More about this later, but this is a *huge* problem in public planning.

Objectives Are Not Quantifiable – While goals can be generally quantifiable, annual objectives must be measurable and time specific. An objective is not 'To *positively impact* the immunization rate among school-age children.' It is not quantifiable and it is impossible to know what this means in terms of increasing immunization rates or reducing the levels of preventable childhood disease in school populations. More accurately, an objective would read, *'To increase, from <65% to >80%, the DPT immunization levels among the K–3 school population.'* Quality strategic plans require measurable objectives that are not confused with activities. The ability to craft reasonable performance/ progress measures is a learned skill that will be more fully discussed in Parts III and IV.

Failing To Raise Key Organization Issues – Properly developed strategic plans encompass review of both external and internal environments. Far too often, there is a unilateral focus on issues within the client base or in the community when many significant issues are internal. Strategic planners *must* consider both dimensions. This is a new concept for most public administrators and elected officials. The historic trend has been to focus analysis and planning on external issues without regarding internal issues that inhibit performance, quality, efficiency, productivity or service delivery. However, without concern for how the organization is performing and developing, your strategic plan will not provide a sustainable platform on which to base program goals or to accomplish its mission.

Not Blending the Mission with Current Issues – An organization's mission must have some root in the issues it addresses. Otherwise, why does it exist? To accomplish what? The organization's *raison d'être* must correspond to the issues, challenges and identified problems in the served community. If it does not, the mission must be revised, or the organization may have outlived its original intent and should be eliminated, restated or assimilated. Some may wonder why this is an element of strategic planning; simply because the genesis of many public services tends to morph over time. This extends some program 'missions' into areas that were not intended by program originators. We have all encountered programs that use general fund or grant dollars to address issues far outside their original missions. Turf expansion is a common feature in any organization, but it is wasteful and inefficient for public agencies to encroach on other public or voluntary organizations whose missions are better aligned with stated issues. If the issues being addressed do not coincide with the organization's stated mission, the mission may be dated or misstated, or the issues are outside the agency's purview. Either way, the plan fails.

The Planning Format Is Too Cumbersome – Keep it simple. Some planning books are so academic and detailed that the processes outlined, though not without merit, are too cumbersome for busy public organizations. As workloads increase public employees must not be burdened with a complex planning process that takes months of meetings, multiple drafts, and endless review.

One of my most memorable discussions was with a county administrator who told me his county had been through several unsuccessful strategic planning attempts. During "far too many meetings over the previous two years, we used dozens of flip chart pads, drank hundreds of gallons of coffee, ate boxes of pastries, but still don't have a written plan." We provided training then facilitated a process that completed a detailed plan in less than eight weeks.

Experience has taught that the best formats have only eight key elements with additional overview sections that provide summations. From the outset, as many employees as practical are trained in the process and continue to remain deeply involved with plan development. This reduces confusion and allows most section, bureau and even division level plans to be completed in less than eight to fifteen pages, emphasizing clarity, brevity and virtually no narratives. Those readers with considerable time in public service have learned that strategic thinking and planning must be simple, clear and meaningful. If it is confusing or overly complex, there will be resistance by those who will work hard to establish a self-fulfilling prophecy that supports the refrain, 'We told you planning would be a waste of time."

Overcoming Resistance to Planning

Planning activities take time away from already busy schedules. As workloads have increased, the resistance to planning has grown due to it being an additional time and energy drain on overburdened employees. Planning must therefore have inherent value, that value must be communicated in meaningful terms, and there must be follow-through.

Value exists in several dimensions. Done well, strategic planning provides the basis for funding because it addresses significant issues and challenges that are important to internal efficiency and for community improvement. It supports prioritization of funding requests that often rely on 'financial triage' for fund allocation. Plans provide clarity about what is important to the agency and community...what the issues are and why they are important. Through their plans, employees can articulate their professional concerns and showcase their program's contribution to the community. Without decent plans, it is often difficult to showcase exactly what is being done, why it is important and what is being accomplished. In addition to previous suggestions, overcoming resistance to planning also requires the following:

- **Communicate the value of planning** – Explain why strategic planning is essential to good government and why it is important for the agency. Announce the strategic planning effort as a key administrative initiative.

- **Train key people properly** – Provide organized, formal training in strategic thinking and plan development; don't launch before training is complete.

- **Remove barriers and provide resources** – Allow ample time and resources to support the planning process.

- **Prepare and distribute planning materials and examples** – Participants always ask to see examples of a properly completed plan; provide samples along with guides, and lay out a systematic process that can be easily followed.

- **Hold sessions to discuss trends and challenges** – Employees always understand the issues an agency, division, bureau or section is facing and typically have accessible data. After training and orientation to the planning process, begin with work sessions to identify major issues and challenges to generate involvement and a feeling of ownership.

It is important to remember that strategic planning is not a panacea for program development or performance. Ultimately, it is a process for improvement, and it is every agency's challenge to clarify those issues and challenges that need remediation. Planning is *not* just a senior management responsibility but needs to be understood and carried out by personnel at all levels. And finally, it is not a one-shot annual process that is completed and shelved for the rest of the year.

Chapter 9

Organizational Outcomes of the Planning Process

In an environment that is 'pre-framed,' that is, structured through years of policy, statute and tradition, properly conducted planning generates many benefits. Regardless of why programs were originally created or their current focus, a thoughtful planning process offers multiple contributions to a public agency or entire government. Among the most important are:

- **Develops a greater degree of cooperation and collaboration** – I am often asked to provide team building programs to voluntary, state and local government agencies. As part of initial conversations, there are questions about how to gain the most from team building events. To the senior official asking the question, my answer might seem surprising. Team building, in my view, fails miserably when presented as a *program*. Very simply, the best way to build a collaborative team is to have individuals work together on something *meaningful*. Ask them to identify issues that affect their program, agency or community and develop strategies that will address those issues. Working together on meaningful assignments, such as a strategic plan, builds teams. Conducting a team building exercise will not have nearly the same impact.

- **Encourages creativity and innovation** – Clearly defined issues and critical challenges have a way of sparking new thought, innovative solutions, and the courage to lead. Once there is understanding about what the agency or community is facing, people move to a higher level of commitment and determination as they explore solutions. As with teambuilding, facilitating opportunities for people to collaborate generates broader, more creative thought and entirely new resource applications.

- **Ensures a more efficient use of resources** – Triage will become more important as resources decline. A properly executed strategic planning process will identify the most compelling issues and challenges facing programs, organizations and communities. Properly written, each issue will contain data that clearly defines its impact—how broadly and deeply that particular issue will affect constituents and stakeholders. Once issues are identified and data is reviewed, elected decision-makers and senior managers can make difficult budget allocation decisions. This helps clarify an agency's intent to provide specific services and how funds will be used. Without each department and individual operating divisions taking time to identify issues and their impact, there is no basis for decisions, opening the door to conflict, confusion, unrest and wasted resources.

- **Creates a sense of mutual accomplishment** – Every government program will have fully examined its mission, vision, values, critical issues, key goals, annual objectives, and chosen strategies. Together, shared plans will elicit greater understanding among agencies about what challenges are being addressed, their various impacts, and how various programs benefit the community. Independent government agencies that battle for resources without an appreciation for what other agencies are facing have little sense of mutual pride. This must change. Government is facing enormous challenges in the next several decades; collaboration and program integration will become more critical.

- **Reduces confusion regarding roles, responsibilities and accountability** – Particularly apparent in government organizations that have not formerly or properly conducted strategic planning, new comparative data illuminates overlap and emphasizes the inherent value of various programs. Let's be clear—there *are* agencies that have overlapping, often redundant programs or missions that replicate outputs. Planning tends to showcase who does what, why it is done, and how work will contribute to the community. For elected officials trying to balance declining revenues with increasing demand, this process is invaluable.

- **Serves as the basis for evaluating employee and program performance** – A proper planning system includes an element of variance reporting that enables departments and individual programs to measure performance against hard criteria. Well-done plans include this capability and encourage annual performance review. Administrators must ultimately answer the question, 'What did the community get for the dollars spent?'

- **Ties the budget to program performance** – As noted above, properly constructed plans have clear measurements that establish the *intent* to produce results for the dollars spent. Based on every program or agency mission, there must be clear *outputs* and anticipated *outcomes* that benefit specific stakeholders or the entire community. Good plans link performance to budgets and annual funding requests can be aligned with an agency's ability to produce desired results.

- **Accelerates the government's or an agency's ability to solve identified issues and challenges** – Proper planning provides illumination; it puts critical issues on the community 'marquee' for all to see. Once showcased, there is always more energy and commitment to address the issue. There tends to be more collaboration, greater disclosure, and higher priority given to identified issues. As in business, things that are measured tend to get done. Similarly, key issues and challenges along with associated goals, annual objectives, and strategies and performance measures will not be ignored.

Whether you are an elected official, appointed administrator or program manager, this range of benefits strategic planning could very well be your most important legacy. By teaching the process to all employees, you will develop a culture of strategic thinkers who consistently seek and expect measured improvement. The foundation laid by properly conducted strategic planning is critical to developing a learning organization that continually adapts to a rapidly changing world.

Part III introduces the process of constructing and articulating a public sector strategic plan. Many of the words will be familiar to you. What you will find different and interesting is the application of those words and why they matter. It is not so important to keep an open mind as it is to understand the difference language makes when developing a meaningful plan for your entire state, city, county, department or program. I'm willing to bet you will be surprised at its simplicity and how a few amendments can make your planning more relevant and much more powerful than ever before.

Part Three

A New Approach to Strategic Thinking and Public Planning

The genesis of my frustration with most public sector strategic plans is that they rarely indicate the path forward or address critical issues. Though virtually all have reasonable content, most, as previously emphasized, are aggregates of operational 'To Do' lists that do not reflect major strategic issues that government, individual agencies or entire communities are facing. Most planning exercises have marginal value due to insufficient clarity, poor metrics, and only a small measure of value for those responsible for implementation. Before this sounds too much like an indictment of all plans, let me also say that the mere intent to develop plans reflects commitment and many positive outcomes still accrue to organizations that follow some form of annual planning.

Strategic thought, when taken as a whole, is a combination of vision, reflection, analysis, honest appraisal, and a willingness to suggest bold action. It requires dedication to look over the horizon, consider the value or possible impact of major events or situations and facilitate collaborative approaches that improve process, product, or quality of life. Some encourage planning for its value as a means of celebrating accomplishments and contributions. Others advocate planning as a management tool that both calculates and ensures measured performance. Many practitioners would merely say strategic planning is the best means of integrating tangible current reality and projected future needs with the conceptual aspirations of a multidimensional community. Good planning deals with the finite while considering the enormously diverse expectations of a nation, state, district, county or city. To say the least, it is important; it is vital; and it is sometimes very difficult.

Part III examines various elements of a strategic plan and the planning process and introduces a proven system that was developed in local and state government agencies expressly for public and community organizations. As mentioned earlier, much of the traditional planning language and ideology remains intact. It is the application and content of various plan elements that are government-specific.

As introduced, the system has several characteristics unique to public agencies. The approach to establishing and stating issues/challenges, goals and objectives is especially targeted to public organizations. Because public strategic planning must be *issue-driven* it is much more important to clearly express issues while defining their impact on the community. Stated properly, issues provide the basis for long-term goals and measurable annual objectives. Understanding the difference between strategies and actions is also valuable and will receive considerable attention in Part IV.

As promised earlier in the Author's Note, I have made an effort to provide examples that minimize narrative throughout Part III. My intent is to provide a concise review that provides the basis for stronger and more meaningful public agency strategic plans. Take some time to reflect as you read this section. Some diagrams and explanations—especially the one in Chapter 11 that reveals the fundamental essence of strategic planning for public agencies—are critical. The approach is quite simple. Those who have followed its reasoning have developed successful plans for many years.

Keep an open mind and remain vigilant for the subtle variations in planning language and process. Words will sound familiar but some elements of the approach will surprise you in how a few small variations can make a huge difference in plan value. Once you have reviewed this section, I encourage you to study your organization's strategic plan. I can already anticipate your surprise and comfort when you realize how a few simple changes will make your plan extraordinarily powerful and meaningful.

Strategic thought, when taken as a whole, is a combination of vision, reflection, analysis, honest appraisal, and a willingness to suggest bold action. It requires dedication to look over the horizon, consider the value or possible impact of major events or situations and facilitate collaborative approaches that improve process, product, or quality of life.

Chapter 10

Old Format, New Approach

Based on what we continue to see across the country, it is time to change how public agencies approach planning. Most of the essential elements are in place but there are variances in perspective that confuse and frustrate. Both format and content need consistency as well as substance. If a meaningful legacy is to be created, planning must be taught to all employees, have a single, simple format, and become an inclusive process. It can no longer be the sole province of senior managers, or ad hoc "strategic planning" teams. It must become an enduring facet of organizational culture, one that provides direction, clarity of purpose, and rationale for programs and services.

As a leader, many of your greatest contributions will be measured by your ability to help the community understand the variety and depth of its challenges and support programs and services that will maintain stability and quality of life. Good process breeds good product; the preferred future of your community is the ultimate product.

As a point of clarity, when I say all employees need to learn planning, I understand that there are often several hundreds or thousands of employees and they cannot possibly all be involved with plan development. To the extent possible, train and involve as many as practical, with representation throughout the organization.

Building a Foundation

There are certain characteristics that add strength and character to public plans. Some are relatively common; others are departures from the norm. All are easy to include and require little new information. As a foundation, it is important to embrace several core characteristics. All strategic planning formats and processes should encompass and/or consider the following:

1. **Identify both internal and external issues**. This is a major departure from historic public planning. However, modern strategic planning *must* deal with both internal (organizational) and external (community) issues. It is natural to focus on only external issues and challenges because they define and reinforce why the agency exists. But without examining the agency, section, bureau or division for internal problems and concerns, only part of the strategic thinking and planning process is complete. Be courageous! Take a hard look at how the program, division or department operates. Is it efficient and effective? Does it have chafing points and internal disharmony that erodes morale, reduces trust and stifles progress? Are the required systems in place, is equipment available, and training offered? Is there adequate capability to achieve the mission? Any of these could be internal factors that inhibit the ability to achieve the mission. Don't be afraid to hold up the mirror and take a hard look—it will pay significant dividends.

2. **Establish a separate, stand-alone plan for each section, bureau, division or department within an organization**. Every element of the larger organization that has a specific mission should be expected to create a brief but complete strategic plan. I believe in accountability and am concerned about any program element that cannot articulate its mission or explain the most pressing needs or issues its services address. Elected officials and appointed administrators must create the expectation that managers down to the section level are able to share a simple plan

that at the very least can describe that unit's mission, key issues and challenges, long-term goals, annual objectives and its action plan for addressing stated issues and achieving described goals. I would be concerned about any standalone entity within state or local government that did not have a plan.

3. **Reduce key information to no longer than five to ten pages** for sub-units (sections and bureaus) and no longer than ten to fifteen pages for major divisions. In other words, there is no reason for a section or bureau plan to be longer than ten pages (although I have seen great section plans that have twelve or fifteen pages). Lose the long narrative—it is unnecessary and cumbersome. Insist on concise, clear and direct plans for every part of the organization. Once they are completed, they can be assembled into an overall agency plan that has an executive summary and specific roll-up sections that summarize the plan for the entire department. If every organization element has a concise plan, the government will have the basis for evaluating performance, contribution and accountability.

4. **Identify major issues that affect that particular organization element and its constituents**. In other words, what critical issues or challenges have been identified that relate to that particular mission? Remember, public agencies for the most part address issues throughout the state or in the local community. Issues create needs within the community and it is these needs that public agencies exist to address. If there were no potholes, crime, disease, fire, license renewals, old infrastructure, growing population, accidents, etc. there would be no need for agencies to address them. The strongest platform of a public sector plan should be the articulation of issues and challenges, because they define and justify why that agency or program exists. If there is no justification, it should not exist. It's that simple. Later, I will address the question of standardized services that have become norms over the years but did not have major issues behind their

A major failing of most strategic plans is that they include a number of actions and tasks that should be kept in an operating plan.

origin (some would debate that). Parks and recreation might be an example. Most parks were created as a public service, not to solve a serious problem. However, now that parks exist, what are the issues associated with operating and maintaining them? What value do parks and recreational programs bring to the community and what issues are associated with providing services (such as growing program demands or insufficient facilities)?

5. **Resist including a lot of operational activities**. As explained earlier, operating and strategic plans are companion documents and together provide an integrated executive approach to public management. In many ways, the strategic plan is a higher level companion document that provides some of the basis for elements found in the operations plan. Quite often, the operations plan contains a variety of operational actions that can be aggregated into action plans that ultimately contribute to strategic goals and objectives. But operations plans describe basic service delivery—little of which is strategic. In the strategic plan it is fine to include some operational actions under objectives, as long as the plan does not become a detailed operations plan. The overview in Part II addressed the differences in these two elements of executive planning. Take time to understand and manage those differences.

6. **Focus on improvement and performance**. As noted earlier, these two factors are the basis for making a difference in the community and in organization management. In terms of leaving a *legacy*, there is the combined benefit of establishing a sound strategic planning process that becomes part of the culture and bringing about significant measurable improvements in productivity and service by addressing identified issues. There would be no reason to plan if there was no need to maintain performance levels or to improve. Accurate issue statements will always provide clarity about what improvements

The strongest platform of a public sector plan should be the articulation of issues and challenges, because they define and justify why that agency or program exists. If there is no justification, it should not exist. It's that simple.

need to be made. Similarly, if an established standard is being achieved, the goal will be to maintain that standard. *Very simply, in government, you are seeking to make internal or external improvements or maintain established internal or external standards.*

7. **Measure improvement in clear, quantifiable outputs and outcomes.** *Everything* can and should be measured and the easiest place to start is with outputs and outcomes. Remember that outputs are generally countable, as in the number of licenses distributed, classes given, immunizations administered, miles of road paved, bridges refurbished, tons of waste recycled, cases worked, etc. An *outcome* is typically the *result* of one or more outputs, such as the reduction of the incidence of reported cases of measles in school-age children. The number of immunizations given is the *output*, and can be counted; the *outcome* is the reduction in disease incidence within the school-age population. It can also be measured but is a *result* of the immunizations. Outputs are generally considered primary elements of operating plans but outcomes are perhaps more important to elected officials and community executives because they demonstrate ultimate results or achievements. For now, keep in mind that outputs and outcomes are found in both strategic and operating plans. The distinction relates to what each addresses (recall that one is typically *mission-driven*, the other is *issue-driven*). For either type of plan, public administrators will achieve enormous success if they are able to execute and measure both outputs and outcomes, based on identified issues within their sphere of responsibility.

Plan Content – Keep It Simple

Simplicity in planning is always a virtue. Long, elaborate plans do no more to clarify strategic intent than plans no longer than ten or twelve pages. Using this system, I have seen bureaus with a hundred and fifty employees and budgets of $5-to-$10-million with strategic plans of less than twelve pages. There are very large departments of 10,000 employees or more that contain large divisions with strategic plans less than twenty pages long. How can it be so brief? Because it deals with only those critical issues that impact the community, immediate stakeholders, or its ability to achieve its mission.

An entire department summary should be a composite, or overview, of the most salient points that have been derived from division and bureau plans, so in turn may be only twenty to thirty pages. For the entire compiled planning document, because separate section, bureau and division plans are compiled into one binder, it may indeed seem large, but will be comprised of many individual plans that stand alone, each presenting its own specific mission, issues, goals, objectives etc. Each independent plan has clear mission and vision statements, a well crafted operating philosophy or statement of values, a list of key issues or problems and perhaps six to twelve properly written goals that establish clear direction. A list of measurable annual objectives for each goal with planned strategies and actions under each allows the reader to know exactly what the bureau or division intends to accomplish. Clear, concise and powerful, this kind of strategic plan will accomplish more than long, involved narrative plans that attempt to portray a variety of operational actions as planned strategic outcomes.

One of your most important legacies is to clarify terminology, provide examples of properly crafted plan elements, explain a sensible planning process and implement it in a way that is meaningful and productive for every facet of your agency.

A plan for a government agency must be a *practical* document that serves as a guide for the organization and a map to help constituents understand what the agency is facing, where its major challenges are, what goals have been established and what actions will be taken to achieve annual objectives. Throughout, there is the assumption that improvement will occur and that identified problems and needs will be successfully addressed. Having only seven or eight sections, a plan using this format will be concentrated and deal with important matters. It will *not* deal with a variety of unrelated operational issues or activities.

The Great Challenge

Though it may be a contentious subject for many elected and appointed officials and staff professionals, the greatest challenge is teaching public employees how plans are written and the difference between a goal, objective, action or strategy. As emphasized previously, most plans have improperly written goals and objectives. Over the past thirty-five years, I have found only a few supervisors and managers at any level who can actually describe the differences between an issue, goal, objective, strategy and action. The same is true of mission and vision statements. Many mission statements are hybrids comprised of misstated missions, visions and value statements, all mixed together. The reason for this is not mysterious. Very few graduate and undergraduate public administration or public affairs programs offer sound courses in a strategic planning system for government. Those that do tend to offer hybrid systems based on planning systems developed for business. There are also very few courses available on the market for practicing elected officials, public administrators or managers that offer accurate training in public sector strategic planning. And, of those available, most tend to focus on overall plan content or format and not the proper articulation of key elements.

As a leader, one of your most important legacies is to clarify terminology, provide examples of properly crafted plan elements, explain a sensible planning process and implement it in a way that is meaningful and productive for every facet of your agency.

Collectively, we are facing a variety of residual and newly emerging challenges that will dwarf previous challenges. Reduced tax revenues are restricting state and local budgets at a time when infrastructure is rapidly deteriorating, costs are escalating and population growth is bringing more service demands. Strategic planning addresses critical issues and challenges. It illuminates the realities being faced by public agencies and details predicted impact. Good plans describe long-term goals and annual objectives that express desired solutions and meaningful outcomes. As a leader, many of your greatest contributions will be measured by your ability to help the community understand the variety and depth of its challenges and to generate support for programs and services that will maintain stability and quality of life. Good process breeds good product; the preferred future of your community is that ultimate product.

A plan for a government agency must be a practical document that serves as a guide for the organization and a map to help constituents understand what the agency is facing, where its major challenges are, what goals have been established and what actions will be taken to achieve annual objectives. Throughout, there is the assumption that improvement will occur and that identified problems and needs will be successfully addressed.

Chapter 11

A New Way of Thinking

Corporations rely on strategic planning to assess markets, competition, and product compatibility. Annual plans chart a course forward and will hopefully provide a sensible guide to destinations defined by margin, retained earnings, and market share. For corporations, planning has moved from very long-term to shorter, more dynamic processes that facilitate adaptation. Nimble business is sustainable business and planning is often the key to both stability and durability.

Public planning is different. For years, planning mavens have tried to shoehorn business planning into annual government strategic planning, promising similar benefits. As suggested earlier, it just doesn't fit. This short chapter explains why. For perhaps the first time, there is a simplified system of strategic thinking that fits government and matches the very purpose and value of public agencies. *If you read and remember no other chapter, I hope you read this one and use the simple model on the next page as a foundation for how you think about strategic planning.* This is not a distillation of a more complex formula. It was developed over twenty-five years ago to convey to elected officials, administrators and managers the most basic, fundamental essence of public sector strategic thinking and planning.

The entire conceptual design of how to think about public strategic planning is found in the following model:

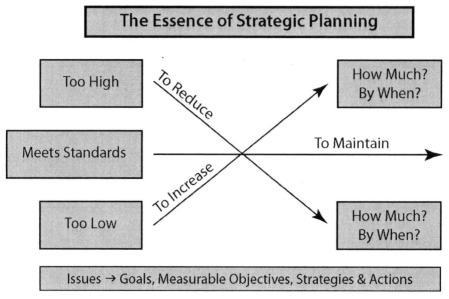

Figure 1.

As you view this simple model, consider the following 'thought path':

1. Issue and Data-Driven

As emphasized several times in this book, business planning is *opportunity* and *tactics* driven; public agency strategic plans must be *issue-driven*. Further, they benefit from and are validated by data. If your issues have clear, accurate data and that data is expressed properly, goals are easy to ascertain, objectives have a basis for measurement, and annual performance metrics have a solid foundation. Therefore, your initial task as a program, division, or agency administrator is to gather all relevant data in various subject categories. For instance, if you are the manager of a public works or utility district water department, gather all pertinent data regarding every phase of the operation. Look at data associated with demand, supply, quality, system age, system failure rates, system pressure, peak use, usage patterns, complaints, and any other pertinent data that is typically monitored.

After you put the data 'on the wall,' you can determine if you are on target, too high or too low. If population growth is creating demand that is growing past the point that supply can be maintained during peak hours, then the goal would be 'To increase supply.' If you determine that there have been too many system failures—greater than your standards allow—then your goal would be 'To reduce the number of system failures.'

In public health, if data indicate that immunization rates are far below acceptable standards recommended by the Centers for Disease Control, the goal would be 'To increase immunization rates.'

Let's say you are responsible for street maintenance and one of the issues identified during a planning session is the number of complaints about potholes. Data indicates that the actual number of potholes in the city has increased by 227% and complaints have tripled. It seems logical that your fundamental goal would be 'To reduce the number of potholes within the city limits.' You have identified the issue, reviewed the data, and determined that the number of potholes is *too high*. Because of the magnitude of the problem, you then decide that this should be one of your key goals. The goal *'To reduce'* provides direction and announces that you are going to address this negative situation.

Hundreds of issue examples can be found in state and local government agencies.

Whether you are involved with health, education, social services, a Clerk's Office, Treasurer, parks and recreation, fire department, law enforcement, utilities, planning, building inspection, human resources, the courts, corrections, wastewater, solid waste, etc. you will be able to utilize this model to review data then determine what is too high, too low and within standards. Some agency managers claim that there is insufficient data to develop issue statements. Frankly, I have never found this to be the case in any

Business planning is opportunity and tactics driven; public agency strategic plans must be issue-driven.

federal, state, city or county agency. There is always data; some is not as accessible or comprehensive as desired, but is ample enough to discern major issues and challenges.

2. A New Thought Process

It is essential to recognize that government exists to serve the broader community. Public organizations address external and internal issues to improve the community and strengthen operating effectiveness. As public administrators, your roles are often defined by your ability to identify important issues and problems, pose solutions, and measure results. Once data on any subject is gathered, it is relatively easy to determine if the indicated numbers are acceptable or unacceptable. *It is truly that simple.* The problem is that most managers tend to generate dozens of nifty actions and strategies, then assume that they provide a 'strategic' approach. Unfortunately, this is not the case. For government, meaningful strategic questions pertain to what issues are creating, or will create, the most damage to all or any element of the community.

For any conceivable topic, once data is available and presented, public managers must answer three questions:

  a. Is this number too high?

  b. Is this number too low?

  c. Is this an acceptable value?

A good strategic thinker concentrates on issues first then determines what the data indicates. Remember, in any department, division, bureau, or work unit, members of that professional team are the subject matter experts. They know the data and can determine what it is telling

As public administrators, your roles are often defined by your ability to identify important issues and problems, pose solutions, and measure results.

them. As suggested previously, if the value is too high, the goal must be *To reduce*; if the value is determined to be too low, the goal must be *To increase*; and, if the value is determined to be within standards and acceptable/target parameters, the goal is *To maintain*. In this way, managers know what values are being maintained according to plans and which are important to sustain. Maintenance goals and objectives (discussed later) provide operating parameters for the organization. They provide operating standards that are strategically important to maintain. Water utilities, wastewater, public health, air quality, public safety, etc. all have critical standards that must be maintained.

Always keep in mind that, if data shows a value is outside acceptable standards, experts (sometimes with input from elected officials) must decide if it is too high or too low. If you find, for instance, that the number of traffic accidents in a downtown city core has *increased* from 27 to 112 in the past five years, your goal might be *To reduce the number of traffic accidents occurring within the downtown city core*. The issue is the growing number of automobile accidents; you have the numbers and have determined that the current number (value) is unacceptable. The goal is therefore 'To reduce...'

Taking an administrative example, let's say that data indicates that it takes a county license bureau an average of 30 minutes to conduct one license renewal transaction. The regional average is less than 18 minutes, so complaints in your area abound. The County Commission has determined, in concert with the License Bureau director, that this number is too high. The goal is therefore 'To reduce...' (We'll discuss objectives later—they have measurement and address the question, 'By how much and by when?') Of course, we assume this issue will warrant funding to establish strategies and actions that will solve the problem and bring transaction times down to acceptable limits. But, without a carefully (and powerfully) stated issue containing accurate data and clear goals that indicate what you plan to achieve, funding may be elusive.

*Data holds the key. To address major strategic issues and establish meaningful goals and objectives that are NOT strategies or activities, **all** properly written public sector goals and objectives must be **To increase**, **To reduce**, or **To maintain** a predetermined value.*

3. Follow the model

The model introduces a simple method of creating a linear progression from issue identification through establishing goals and objectives. Once these are established, it is relatively easy to determine strategies and actions, which express *how* you plan to achieve goals and objectives.

Example: Law Enforcement

The agency is the city Police Department, detective bureau. During a work session, it was determined that there are too many open, unsolved cases and that the backlog has grown by 63% in just three years without significant population growth. That is the issue (one of several). As the numbers are shared among the group, the question is posed, 'Is this acceptable?' *No*, the group responds. There is agreement that the number of unsolved, open cases is *too high*, so the goal is *To reduce the number of unsolved open cases*. That is all managers need to establish...that is what they are going to work on—reducing the number of unsolved cases. It does not need to explain *how* it will be accomplished (strategy or action); it merely establishes a direction based on their assessment of the issue.

Keep in mind that goals and objectives do not cost anything; it is strategies and actions that require funding.

The litmus test for goals is simple: If the mayor or a city council member asked one year (or three years) later, 'Did you reduce the average number of unsolved cases?' The answer is either yes or no. You have tracked your progress and have the numbers. The goal was to reduce...either you did or didn't.

The model allows a work team, bureau, division, or department to identify critical issues then explore the data associated with each. Subject matter experts will very quickly determine if the data is within various posted standards, is too high or too low. If too low, the goal is '*To increase;*' if too high, the goal is '*To reduce.*' It typically takes a very short time to review data, establish issues and determine general goals.

Defining Objectives

Once it is clear that a value is too high or too low, the model asks, '*By how much and by when?*' These questions lead to the formation of measurable objectives. Why this has been such a mystery for so long is beyond me. If the goal is '*To reduce* the number of unsolved cases,' the *objective is merely a more precise statement that includes measurement and time* (typically an annual budget cycle.)

What do the data say? If there are currently 112 unsolved cases and this number has been determined as being unacceptably high, the bureau's *goal* is to reduce this number. The objective states that within one year the bureau intends to reduce the number of unsolved cases from 112 to <85 cases—the best they feel they can do in one annual cycle with available resources. *As a statement, the objective mirrors the goal: To reduce, from 112 to <85, the number of open unsolved cases in the detective bureau by ___ (end of the next fiscal year).* They are still reducing but now have inserted a numeric performance measure, 112 to <85 cases. Again, data holds the key. If you have the numbers and they are stated as part of the issue, writing objectives is easy.

In any department, division, bureau, or work unit, members of that professional team are the subject matter experts. They know the data and can best determine what it is telling them.

Most agencies stray from this path because they insert a list of activities and label them goals or objectives. An objective is **not** '*To fund overtime for detectives to enable them to devote more hours on open cases,*' or '*To install new software that simplifies and expedites recordkeeping.*'

Clearly, these are strategies (and not very good ones!). These are solutions that tell *how* the bureau is approaching the issue. Neither is a measurable objective that can be assessed as an element of annual performance.

For some, this will be a departure from plans that do not provide detailed issue/challenge statements from which goals can be generated to express the intent to increase, reduce or maintain. As repeatedly stressed throughout this book, the most significant issue with public sector strategic plans is the lack of powerfully stated, data-driven issues and improperly stated goals and objectives.

This simple model provides a path to follow and results in clear, linear, performance-based plans. As you become familiar with the model, the following chapters provide more detail about how issues, goals, objectives, and strategies/actions are crafted. Many examples are provided and the linear relationship between goals and objectives is more fully explored.

Before leaving this initial introduction to the essence of public sector strategic planning, I want to share the metaphor below. I use it to help planning participants visualize the landscape in which they operate. It is an illustration that has helped many public agency managers understand the relationship that exists among issues, goals, objectives and actions.

Best Planning Metaphor – Football

Picture the planning landscape as a football field, with clearly marked five and ten yard lines the length of the field, and yard markers dividing each five-yard increment. As you look downfield, imagine you are trying to reach the goal line at the other end of the field. It is in the distance, but it is your ultimate *goal* and destination.

Because you are now on your own ten-yard line, you have ninety yards to go to achieve that goal. From a planning standpoint, you realize that, due to insufficient resources, you cannot get to the goal during this fiscal year. So, with the resources available, you determine how far you can move downfield during the year. Because you believe you can move thirty yards toward the goal, that becomes your annual *objective*. You know what the goal is and have established a shorter-term objective that is measured by the yard markers. You can then measure your performance toward the longer-term goal. You may exceed or fall short of the thirty-yard objective and will assess progress at the end of the year, recalibrating as necessary for the next annual cycle. The "plays" you call to move downfield are your *strategies* and *actions*. Hopefully, they will be effective and move you briskly downfield. Typically, some will work, some won't (related to appropriateness, efficiency and effectiveness). Your play calling is your management and it impacts whatever progress is made in dealing with the issue.

The football field provides a metaphor for setting longer-term goals and shorter-term objectives that will move you closer as you proceed downfield. As you plan, see the field and imagine how you will move toward your goals. Progress toward the goal is in measured increments and every yard of progress requires strategies and planned actions—just like football.

Part Four

Building a Public Agency Strategic Plan – Content, Format and Language

There does not seem to be as much confusion about *what* goes into a strategic plan as there is about *how* each section is actually written. As with many things, articulation of intent and process is where people differ and where there has been significant divergence over the past forty years. In my view, the RAND Corporation provided the best guidance in strategic thinking and planning during the mid-1960s, continuing through the 1970s. Planning offered by this very sophisticated organization was clear, concise and relevant to government. But it was also offered in very few venues that would enable it to be imbedded into public agency culture so had minimal impact on general planning expertise. During the intervening years, a hodgepodge of planning theories and styles have emerged, most with genesis in business theory that has little relevance to public agency challenges or culture.

The overarching fact to remember is that government is *not* business. To be sure, it can be managed in a business-like manner, but it is not private enterprise. What motivates public administrators is not (let's hope) what motivates business people. As a public manager, your commitment is serving the public; you are obligated and committed to operating efficiently but are also motivated by the opportunity to leave the legacy of a strong, safe, prosperous community for those who follow. Above all, you are driven to serve the public interest. Strategic thinking and planning are tools in your tool kit. Learn the process and it will provide greater leverage as new challenges emerge and current issues become more severe.

Understanding Each Element

There are only seven or eight sections in an efficient plan. When initially composed, the first three—Mission, Vision and Operating Philosophy (or Values), should take less than one page. Even though they will be formatted for an attractive presentation later (some even framed) the initial work takes a page or two.

The Mission, Vision and Operating Philosophy (Values) should be followed by a properly articulated list of the most significant issues and challenges the bureau, division, department, district or government is facing. Using the issue as a platform, the next section provides long-term goals; and for each goal there is a list of the most important annual measurable objectives that relate to key achievements planned for that one- or two-year budget cycle. Each objective is followed by a list of strategies and actions that will be undertaken to accomplish the objective. I typically encourage every agency that develops a standalone plan to include a list of any major 'strategic initiatives' that the organization wants to get on the radar screen for decision-makers and the budget office. Strategic initiatives are major activities that will take significant time and effort, and are important to the agency and community.

As explained earlier, a well-crafted and concise strategic plan for most bureaus or divisions will take an average of eight to fifteen pages. Anyone reading the plan will understand very quickly the mission, vision, values, major issues/challenges, long-term goals, annual objectives and strategies/actions. Plus, if there are any major initiatives that need to be undertaken, they will be reviewed and briefly explained.

Every element in a public organization that has a distinct reason to exist should have a plan. More critically, every individual part of an agency, whether section, bureau or division, should understand its mission and be able to clearly describe challenges it is addressing, what improvements it plans to make and how. Even if the organization is a standard service, such as parking control, license bureau, risk management, personnel, park maintenance, etc. it will have issues and challenges that may involve its client base (demand) or its own internal effectiveness or efficiency (growing workload, archaic policies, insufficient staff, inadequate equipment, insufficient training). Stated issues provide the basis for improvement and can be addressed in goals and objectives. The message for public agencies is that every unit that has a mission (purpose) must be involved with planning and be expected to have a standalone plan.

Typical Plan Elements

1. Mission
2. Vision
3. Operating Philosophy (Values)
4. Major Issues/Challenges
5. Long-term Goals
6. Annual (or bi-annual) Measurable Objectives
7. Strategies/Actions
8. Major Strategic Initiatives

The above listing is traditional. Those who have been involved with planning will recognize these classic headings. For now, focus on content and how each section is formed and articulated. Later, I will take some time to discuss formatting, which is often based on personal preference or historic internal standards. At this point, be less concerned about a plan's format than about its content. There are many ways to present information, but if the content is poor, the plan will be poor, regardless how attractive.

The following chapters are dedicated to reviewing each plan element, providing examples and explaining various nuances. For many, there will be common threads that affirm what you have learned from past reading and experience. I anticipate, however, that many will find encouragement and encounter some Ah Ha! moments as you begin to understand important differences between goals and objectives and strategies and actions. For others, reviewing each plan element will open new horizons for developing your own plans using a sensible, simple approach.

The message for public agencies is that every unit that has a mission (purpose) must be involved with planning and be expected to have a standalone plan. This should be an expectation of the job and a primary accountability of all managers.

Chapter 12

Defining Mission, Vision and Values

Because mission, vision, and values statements are created once and rarely altered, it is best to discuss them together. All three are therefore presented in this chapter with several examples of each.

These elements are surrounded by myth and misunderstanding. For so many plans, missions are erroneous statements expressing an idealistic vision or presenting an abundance of warm, fuzzy values. Many are hybrid statements that offer no real clarity about any of the three subjects, or so little that one has to interpret their meaning. The same is true with vision statements. I see many vision statements that are loaded with values that have little or nothing to do with what the agency sees in the future or aspires to. Taken separately, mission, vision and values statements are quite straightforward and can be developed with minimal time investment. And, done well, these three plan elements will reveal a great deal about the organization and provide a platform for other more dynamic sections.

I elected to include all three in this chapter because together they provide a strategic plan's introduction to the organization. They present why the organization exists and what it does (mission), explain its view of the future (vision), and express its values in a manner that creates a deeper understanding of its operating philosophy. Each statement is short, concise, and specific to that particular part of the overall organization. I recommend that, at least initially, every element of a department, such as divisions and bureaus, have standalone missions, visions, and values statements. Later, if the director elects to have one statement of values or a vision for the entire agency, that is permissible. But initially, there is great benefit in having each organizational element take time to develop these plan sections. Once crafted, they are reviewed but not revised annually. Unless there are major changes, they should remain constant for many years.

The Mission

For public agencies, the Mission answers two questions, '*Why* does this part of the organization exist? And, '*What* does it do?' A well-written mission statement will answer these questions in from two to five sentences. Again, the most common mistake is to combine elements of vision and values into mission statements. The mission must be clear, concise and straightforward. It helps the reader understand what the department, division or bureau exists to do and generally, *what it does*. As with any professional public document, it does *not* have personal pronouns such as *we* or *our*. This is a common mistake of plan writers. You are not writing a personal story; you are preparing a crisp, professional public document. Expressed in your plan, I prefer to label this section as 'Mission' rather than 'Mission Statement' or 'Statement of Mission.' The same is true with the vision; it is best to call it a 'Vision' and not a 'Vision Statement.' These are extra, unnecessary words. Merely introducing the section as 'Mission' is sufficient. A small thing, but the fewer words the better.

It should be noted that the Armed Services have a different definition of 'mission.' For a military operation, the mission is similar to a broad objective. For example, a military mission might be to 'Liberate the city of Marjah from the Taliban.' The intent is to take over the city, drive out insurgents and return the city to local authorities. These types of tactical missions are not to be confused with public agency missions created to reflect why the agency exists and briefly explain what it does. Every mission statement must therefore do exactly that; a reader must receive adequate information that provides a high level of clarity. After someone reads your mission, they should understand your *raison d'être*—why the organization exits, why it is there and what it does. After all, public agencies have a *purpose* and were created to *do something.* What exactly is it?

Below are several examples taken from existing state or local government strategic plans. Notice that some present the mission in one sentence, while others take two or more. My encouragement is to be concise and accurate but be complete. Also note that the statements do *not* begin with 'The mission of the bureau/department is to...' There is no reason to unnecessarily restate these phrases. You may read these and feel you would reduce their length or word them differently. However, these were prepared by employees in their respective organizations and they liked what they wrote. The key is whether the statement explained the mission clearly and concisely. Notice that each begins with an answer to the question, '*Why* does this organization exist?' And continues to answer the question, 'What does this organization *do?*'

Also, avoid mottos and slogans. They are *not* mission statements. *To Protect and Serve* sounds good but is not a mission. It is a great slogan. Beware trying to distill a mission into a short, but often trite, sentence or phrase. The typical reader is uninitiated to your organization. The mission is written to provide an understanding, not to create a unique slogan or frame-worthy 'catch-phrase.' Those who espouse having a mission statement distilled into a short sentence so it can be memorized by employees are off the mark. A public agency mission must convey a complete message to the public and to decision-makers. It is not meant to be memorized by employees so they can become proficient in giving 'elevator speeches.'

Example #1: Human Resource Development (state agency)

Mission

Human Resources provides training and development leadership to support and enhance the Department's overall continuous improvement efforts, as well as the growth and development of individual employees through consultation, advocacy, technical support, and innovative, effective and efficient training programs.

Example #2: Human Resource Development (city department)

Mission

Human Resources provides leadership and professional consultation as a strategic business partner to help each City department achieve its mission, goals and objectives. Human Resources proactively seeks to understand and meet the needs of its customers, elected officials, Mayor, managers and City employees by providing expertise, direction, support, and training in the areas of recruitment, policies, benefits, compensation, employee relations and staff development while ensuring a safe, fair, and legally compliant work environment.

Example #3: State Highway Operations and Programming

Mission

To provide the department and the public with a realistic and reliable five-year schedule for developing highway improvement projects that effectively and efficiently utilize available transportation funds. The section establishes and directs project scheduling, guides and analyzes project submission, communicates policies and procedures, coordinates staff review and management/Board approval of all project funding requests, and maintains concise records of all funding decisions.

Example #4: City Street Maintenance

Mission

Street Maintenance Operations provides leadership, management, professional/technical expertise, and operating services to efficiently and responsibly preserve the City's streets, rights-of-way, and drainage systems at the highest possible level of safety and reliability.

Example #5: City Finance Department

Mission

To provide leadership and guidance in financial management by utilizing generally accepted standards applicable to financial audits and applying appropriate new technology. The central purpose is to provide professional and accurate financial management of Departmental funds and to provide accounting services to support and promote the successful completion of Departmental goals, meeting requirements of rate resolutions/ordinances, bond covenants, industry standards, and generally accepted accounting standards. In every function, employees model excellent customer service, public awareness, timely response, and accountable financial management.

Example #6: Watershed Management

Mission

To provide leadership and guidance in watershed management by utilizing new technology and ecologically based engineering and planning practices. The Division improves water quality, manages storm water, reduces flood hazards, and insures that the City meets Federal requirements relative to storm water quality. Programs include watershed master planning, storm water education, water quality monitoring, enforcement of adopted standards, and the implementation of storm water capital projects within the City and its future growth areas. The Division encourages sustainable growth by upholding responsible standards that maximize safety, minimize flood damage and conserve natural resources to ensure quality of life for future generations.

Example #7: City Police Department

Mission

To provide the highest quality service in partnership with the community to preserve and protect life and property through education, prevention, and enforcement.

Example #8: Administrative Services (city)

Mission

Administration serves as the central communications, planning, and resource development entity for the agency. The Administrative team seeks and allocates resources, initiates new programs, coordinates and implements agency planning, guides public interaction and collaboration with other community agencies, and continually strives to enhance the ability of agency departments to achieve program goals and objectives.

Example #9: City Fire Department

Mission

The Fire Department protects the life, health, and property of all citizens within the combined urban and rural service area. In addition to rapid response to fire, medical, and other emergencies, the department provides skilled emergency care, public education, code enforcement, structure inspection, hazard analysis, and requested public safety services to the people and organizations that live, visit or operate in this community.

Example #10: Special Education (state agency)

Mission

The Bureau of Special Education was created to improve social and academic results for all children with special needs while promoting quality education and equal educational opportunities for all students. Through its advocacy, equitable distribution of resources, and technical assistance the bureau empowers and supports administrators, educators, and parents in their efforts to prepare all children to lead rewarding, productive lives.

Example # 11: Parks and Recreation (city)

Mission

Parks and Recreation enhances the community's quality of life by providing well-designed and properly maintained parks and recreational opportunities for all citizens. Services include development and maintenance of parks, sport fields, pathways, playgrounds, picnic shelters, and memorials in addition to developing and offering a wide variety of group and individual recreational programs.

There are hundreds of good examples of sensible missions – some better than others – but the best follow the guidelines outlined above. As you begin developing a mission, consider beginning your work session with the sentence, "This unit (department, division, bureau) exists to..." Or, first list the essential services the unit provides to the community or other agencies, then craft into a statement. Ultimately, a mission should explain precisely why the organization exists, then share information about what it does. Because the mission is the opening plan section, it should leave the reader with a clear understanding of the agency, division, bureau or section. Regardless of the government organization being represented, it should present a short, clear explanation.

In the examples above, each typically begins with one sentence that addresses why the organization exists. Sentences that follow generally describe what it does. There is no editorial explanation about rationale or any other extraneous data. There are no confusing values or visionary comments mixed into these statements. They are quite businesslike and exist to convey a simple message. Every element of every government, whether city, county, state or federal, must be able to clearly express its mission. While on this subject, take a few minutes to review your agency's strategic plan or other planning document. How comfortable are you with your organization's mission statement?

The Vision

A public agency vision is very different than those found in private business. Many of those seen framed on the walls in large and small corporations are grand statements of accomplishment and futuristic idyllic conditions. Many public agencies have fallen into the habit of offering similar visions that never come true and lose their energy before the ink has dried. How many times have agencies gone through the planning process and created beautiful, sweeping visions that no one believes can be accomplished?

I contend that public agency visions are different. They *must* be practical and based on a realistic assessment of what the future will bring in terms of challenge and opportunity. While it may be fine to articulate a grand outcome as part of your vision, it must have substance and a high likelihood of completion. Keep in mind that you are here to serve the public interest. You are also here to have thoughtful visions that articulate hopes and dreams of the future, but not by sacrificing practicality. As a public servant, you are responsible for offering a professional assessment of the future; in other words, your vision.

Let me expand on the previous comment. I have encountered many officials that insist on a utopian vision—something to aspire to. When confronted with an insistent official or administrator, I offer a different perspective. As a professional, you and your peers are the best resources to articulate the vision for an agency or any of its component parts. If a citizen, council member, commissioner, or legislator asked you to describe what you see coming that might impact the community or your stakeholders, what would you say? *You* are the professional with the experience, knowledge and data. You are the subject matter expert. Your vision should not be based on illusory conjecture that portrays a La-La Land destination. It must be grounded in fact and clear data.

Very simply then, a public sector Vision is a *practical* statement about the future and the organization's role in it. It is an opportunity to look forward, to check prospective viewpoints and to clearly explain what the organization sees coming. The future and vision should not be judged as positive or negative—it just is what it is. The best vision is also a brief statement that expresses what the agency will, or may, do to meet predicted challenges. A third element may describe an *ideal desired outcome*, such as *'Crime rates half the national average within ten years,'* but the first two elements are more critical. It is essential that public vision statements be thoughtful assessments of the future, based on sound research and professional judgment (are you willing to say *'Crime-free streets within ten years?'*) It is also important to review for the reader the general plans the agency has to meet the future as described. The reader wants to know. Tax money is supporting the program and there is little patience for grand statements or flowery language. Like the Mission, *the Vision contains no personal pronouns*; it is straightforward, clear and as precise as possible.

As you begin developing a vision, consider these questions:

1. As a professional what do you see coming at your agency and the community over the next several years?

2. What efforts will the agency make to address, avoid, or counter the predicted variables?

When reading the examples, remember that these came from programs that went through deliberations to identify an assortment of variables that employees feel will impact the organization. Some also express in general terms how the organization plans to address those circumstances and variables.

Public agency visions are different. They must be practical and based on a realistic assessment of what the future will bring in terms of challenge and opportunity. While it may be fine to articulate a grand outcome as part of your vision, there certainly better be substance behind it and a high likelihood of completion.

Example #1: Administrative Services (state agency)

Vision

During the coming decade, the section will experience increased work volume, more demand for diverse and complex services and greater centralization in an environment characterized by limited resources and a trend toward service integration. General Services will continue to be the leader in acquiring and utilizing technology to achieve greater efficiency and cost-effectiveness, and will invest in professional training to develop expertise to meet the growing business needs of the department.

Example #2: Police Department (city)

Vision

During the next decade the Police Department will adapt to an increasingly diverse and expanding community through collaborative planning, more efficient operations and individual professional development. The department anticipates that community crime, safety and security concerns will grow with population, diversity and economic challenges and demands for police services will increase. The department will emphasize careful planning, utilizing all available resources to remain effective and responsive to issues concerning public safety and crime.

Emphasis will be on enhancing and fostering collaborative partnerships with the community and with other public service agencies; encouraging and maintaining a commitment to individual professional development that stresses education, training, and ethical standards; continual review of needs and concerns within the community and department; and proactive interaction through planned activities and programs directed at enhancing public safety, crime prevention and risk reduction.

Example # 3: Finance Department

Vision

The City will continue to experience population growth, which will create additional demand for more and better financial information, financial planning and analysis. Increased accounting and reporting capability will be required of all departments, as will timely, more pro-active and accurate reports, better historic accounting, and more specific, detailed analysis for both the public and city officials. New and more complex challenges will be met through sound accounting procedures and systems utilizing modern computing capability and analysis tools, and offering financial training to all departments to promote higher quality record keeping, better collaboration, and adherence to proper financial standards.

Example # 4: City Clerk

Vision

The next decade will continue to bring commercial and residential growth, creating broader and more complex demands on public services, and stressing the 'small town' culture that has been the City's most enduring characteristic. Citizen expectations will grow along with urban boundaries, bringing opportunities to disconnect at a time when a sense of community is more critical than ever. To meet the challenge, the City Clerk's Office will promote better public information, seek a centralized, more visible city hall/municipal center, offer greater public accessibility, and embrace the wise use of technology to provide new efficiencies, services and opportunities for citywide cooperation.

Example # 5: City Human Resources

Vision

Recognizing the future growth of the City, HR will work as a strategic partner with management by proactively recruiting, retaining, and motivating high-performance employees to enhance organizational effectiveness in meeting City objectives and demands. To meet increased growth and challenges HR will implement strategic programs of recruitment, performance management, management development, employee orientation and create new tracking systems. It will use new technologies to achieve greater efficiencies, streamline processes, enhance policy effectiveness, and improve City compliance with labor law and compensation strategies.

Example # 6: City Parks and Recreation

Vision

The department anticipates continued population growth within the service area, bringing escalating and more concentrated demand at a time when funds are limited, outdoor facilities remain insufficient, and support for indoor facilities will lag behind community needs. To ensure the best possible use of resources as public demand grows, the department will seek creative options to build facilities and offer new programs through private- public partnerships, by utilizing grant funds, and promoting collaboration with service agencies to provide exceptional parks and recreational programs for the community.

Example # 7: Planning and Zoning

Vision

Based on community trends, the future will be characterized by more complex and diverse developments, integrated mixed-use and socio-economic areas, a broader business and economic base, greater overall density, more demand for open space within developments, and a constantly growing population.

To meet emerging challenges, the department will seek new efficiencies through electronic technology, better public and professional education, updated ordinances that support the community's vision, stronger incentives for 'performance-based' developments, and clear data that can guide decisions by elected officials. Through its work, the department will help create a community with a sustainable 'small town' atmosphere, a positive, progressive image, and a reputation for prudent, harmonious growth.

Notice how each vision is an unembellished statement about the future and what the writers felt it would bring. This is what they would say if asked their views on what they believe the future will hold—what challenges will come. As with all such statements, you may not agree with either the viewpoint or how it is expressed. However, it is the product of a group of experienced professionals from various public agencies and represents true feelings and their assessment of what they see coming. This type of vision statement is a treasured element of the overall strategic plan, but is not written to be framed and exhibited in the lobby. Citizens and elected officials need and want straightforward viewpoints regarding what their professional departments see coming.

As strategic thinkers, I encourage you to embrace this more practical definition of a Vision. Discussions surrounding the development of a vision statement are by themselves priceless. They will generate dialogue that would otherwise not occur. From experience in many venues, I can attest that some of the best discussions have occurred while developing a sensible, fact-driven vision.

When confronted with an official or administrator who insists on an ideal vision, I offer a different perspective. As a professional, you and your peers are the best resources to articulate the vision for an agency or any of its component parts. If a citizen, council member, commissioner, or legislator asked you to describe what you see coming that might impact the community or agency stakeholders, what would you say? YOU are the professional with the experience, knowledge and data; you are the subject matter expert. What if the facts portray a more sobering and challenging vision? Why would you state otherwise?

Operating Philosophy or Statement of Values

When working with groups I look forward to the time spent on values and am always surprised by how few administrators take time to discuss these basic organization cornerstones. What is more important than your values? They provide the behavioral parameters for virtually every aspect of management, yet are often neglected. I find this curious.

Termed "Values Statement" in many plans, I offer the term *Operating Philosophy* because I believe it connotes a statement about what a team believes about its work, desired attitudes and interpersonal behavior. It expresses how employees treat each other, their clients, stakeholders and the community. It is a much stronger statement than one that merely lists values. While based on a set of values, it is also based on identified adjectives that the work team feels best describes them and the organization's culture. A good test is to ask, 'If someone from outside the organization was to describe this team, what adjectives would they use? What characteristics would you *want* them to cite when describing the organization? As a team, what do *you* believe about the value of your work and what are you committed to?' By developing an Operating Philosophy or Values Statement, employees will have identified the organization's essential values. Importantly, *it is the only section in a strategic plan in which personal pronouns are appropriate,* because it is a personal statement by that particular group of employees or the employees of the entire agency.

As suggested earlier, very few organizations take the time to discuss an operating philosophy. While the traditional method is to convene one or more 'focus groups' to identify values, defining the organization's operating philosophy takes more thought and results in clear behavioral standards and expectations. I term these 'covenants' because the team agrees on them and establishes them as central cultural guidelines. Taking time to establish a philosophy that defines how the team acts and serves the public is an important and enduring legacy.

Below is an example of one organization's listing of adjectives that the members feel defines it as an intact work group. It also became the foundation of its Operating Philosophy and had remarkable long-term impact on the group's harmony and productivity.

Our bureau demonstrates and/or believes in ...

- Commitment to managed change
- Belief in the value of every individual
- Commitment to collaborate, communicate and cooperate
- Dedication to service, response, closure, friendliness
- Deep belief in integrity, honesty, openness, courage
- Respect for diverse cultures, tolerance, work integration
- Concern for people, property and preservation of standards
- Focus on commitment, initiative, pride, spirit, teamwork and harmony

Similar to the Vision, the Operating Philosophy should be a fairly concise statement that captures the essence of the group's beliefs and culture. It is rarely over three sentences long and five sentences should be the limit. Long statements quickly lose their impact while short slogans or mottos do not appropriately depict values.

The major complaint about operating philosophies or statements of values is that they may sound too mushy or idealistic. Frankly, that may be true. However, the purpose of the process is to provide employees with an opportunity to identify and discuss personal and organization values and express them in terms that resonate. They are *not* writing them to be framed (although some are beautifully formatted and placed on the wall) and are certainly not conducting the exercise to placate citizens or justify programs or services. The purpose is to understand and articulate how the organization feels about its work, its commitments and obligations; further, it clarifies in writing what the organization is as an entity—as a collection of dedicated public servants.

If, as you read the examples, you feel some are overstated or too ethereal, that is perfectly acceptable. My encouragement is to take time to identify *your* organization's values and express them in a statement that expresses *your* operating philosophy and defines your culture. It may explore terrain that is unfamiliar to you, but that is healthy.

The following all came from state and local government agencies:

Example #1: Office of Civil Rights

Operating Philosophy

We believe in a work environment and programs characterized by consistency, honesty, responsiveness, discretion and trust. We are concerned, committed professionals who are straightforward, determined and adaptable in a rapidly changing environment. Above all, we respect our internal and external customers, and maintain for them the highest possible standards of fairness and impartiality.

Example #2: Division of Public Transportation

Operating Philosophy

We believe in being helpful, reliable, open, honest, accessible, responsive, and well-informed. We are problem solvers who believe in teamwork and personal commitment, and pay particular attention to cost-effectiveness and fiscal responsibility. We have respect and appreciation for the public and are dedicated to providing safe, accessible, convenient and sensible public and private transportation choices for all who live in and visit our community.

Example #3: City Clerk

Operating Philosophy

We are a conscientious, hard-working, and honest team dedicated to providing accessible, accurate services to all public agencies, businesses and citizens. We take great pride in our work and are committed to the ideals of open communication, integrity and accountability. Above all, we appreciate the opportunity to serve this community and do so in a manner that protects the public trust, preserves our quality of life and promotes economic prosperity.

Example #4: City Finance Department

Operating Philosophy

We are a knowledgeable and highly organized team dedicated to exceptional customer service characterized by courtesy, accuracy, and reliability. We are committed to providing timely and accurate financial services in an efficient, responsive, and consistent manner that enables each City department to wisely manage and effectively use limited resources to provide quality services to citizens. Above all, we are a conservative group that takes its financial responsibilities seriously and enjoys a reputation for being practical, helpful, and professional.

Example #5: Fire Department

Operating Philosophy

We are a skilled and resourceful professional team known for high integrity, compassion, and dedication. Both as individuals and as a department, we are caring, trustworthy, and steadfast in our willingness to meet any challenge associated with maintaining a safe, secure, and prepared community.

Example #6: Parks and Recreation

Operating Philosophy

We are a caring, creative, and hard-working professional team dedicated to providing meaningful recreational services to the community. As public employees, we believe in meaningful collaboration with others and are committed to sharing our experience, knowledge, and resources with all who support and/or participate in services that promote good health and exceptional quality of life.

Example #7: Public Works

Operating Philosophy

The Public Works Department is a progressive, highly productive professional team dedicated to providing customer service in a manner that is courteous, prompt, and thorough. We believe in this community and embrace the responsibility to serve and protect the public trust while performing to very high standards of fiscal accountability, personal integrity, honesty, and fairness.

Example #8: College of Education (university)

Operating Philosophy

We hold the interests of public school students as our core value. As a dedicated team, we collaborate to provide a dynamic and caring environment for pre- and in-service teachers interested in improving the educational lives of public school children.

Example #9: Counseling Department (university)

Operating Philosophy

> As a highly ethical professional team, we are competent, respectful, and responsive counselor educators who maintain an adaptive environment that is educationally challenging and supportive of all students and colleagues. We believe in consensus in a nurturing and collaborative department that promotes academic rigor, professionalism, and quality student outcomes.

Notice how these work teams stated their beliefs, using adjectives that they felt define the organization. For new employees, these statements provide clear parameters that reflect the culture and characterize the belief system; they also establish expectations related to attitude, commitment, and behavior. Yet, it took only a few sentences and most are not overly flowery. Importantly, it is *their* statement about *their* work unit and they believe it. While others may read these examples and suggest changes, it is best to let each work group create their own operating philosophy or values statement because they have to live with and by it. This is another example of the *process* being more important than the *product*.

An Operating Philosophy or Values Statement is the ONLY section in a strategic plan in which personal pronouns are appropriate, because it is a personal statement by that particular group of employees or of the employees of the entire agency.

The Process

It is human nature to judge examples developed by others and this is one of the difficulties of sharing plans from other city, county and state agencies. When training begins for a group of administrators and managers, early dialogue tends to center around what others wrote rather than the importance of identifying values and how those managers philosophically manage their agencies. My advice is to not judge the examples. Get a feel for the process and how understanding your own values can contribute to your agency. Here are several suggestions that will make this part of planning enjoyable and productive:

1. Every independent organization element having a specific mission should take time to develop a set of values and craft into an operating philosophy.

2. Convene a good cross section of employees into a working group that will identify values and create a draft. For large organizations, a brief survey also works well.

3. As a group, begin by identifying key adjectives that define the organization. Start by asking, 'What defines us? What are the *attributes* of this team, section, bureau, division or department that can be stated as values? How would we complete the sentence, 'As a group, we are ____?' Think of adjectives that define you and that characterize your spirit, commitment, attitude, style, culture, etc. Do this in a short, intense session that lasts no longer than thirty minutes.

4. Once you have developed a good list, use multiple voting or some other decision-making method to select the top adjectives or characteristics; a list of six to ten is typical, although statements with more than ten are not uncommon. Note the number and type of adjectives in the examples. (It is easy to picture the list each group used to develop a final statement.)

5. Prepare a draft Values Statement/Operating Philosophy and share with other employees, asking for their input and suggested amendments. Depending on organization size, it may be impossible to share with all employees. In that case, share with various work units and require that managers share ideas and solicit suggestions from as many employees as possible.

6. After all input is gathered, wordsmith a final statement and share with employees. As with all planning activities, share widely and retain an open process. To the extent possible, create an enduring statement that will not have to be revised in coming years. The

better it matches and defines the culture the more durable and valuable it will be.

If you are an administrator, the work invested in developing your values statement or operating philosophy may be the best and most productive time you ever spend. I encourage managers to use these statements in recruiting, new employee orientation, and employee development programs. It is a message that expresses who you are and what you stand for. Please don't take the process lightly. Once you complete the process and the final statement, it will be seen as a reflection of the organization and will present to the world a snapshot of your organization's spirit.

Summary – Mission, Vision, Operating Philosophy

Properly written, these three plan sections will take less than a page apiece, but taken together, they will introduce the organization. The Mission explains *why* the agency or unit exists and what it does. It clarifies the organization's purpose in clear, concise sentences.

The Vision presents an opportunity to share what you see coming at the agency—the challenges or changing circumstances that the community will contend with in the future. In my view, it is a statement crafted by professional subject matter experts that the community relies on for expertise and foresight. What challenges do you see on the horizon and how, generally, do you plan to address them? Beware being too ethereal or utopian. The future will be a challenging place and the last thing elected officials or the community needs is a bunch of hooey based on someone's version of an ideal world. Be practical and thoughtful. That is not to say you cannot include a statement that defines hoped-for status or a desired outcome. Just don't get too idealistic in the face of reality. If the reader cannot accept the stated outcome because it is so disconnected from reality, the plan and agency will lose credibility.

Finally, the Operating Philosophy represents your values and provides a definition of your culture. It clarifies what you believe, how you behave, and how your values are applied through your work as public servants. Take time to craft a strong statement. It is yours. It is what you are as an agency…or a community.

Chapter 13

Identifying Major Issues and Challenges

This chapter provides the 'epicenter' of strategic plan development because issues and challenges are the launching point for all public plans.

It introduces the most fundamental difference between public sector operations planning and strategic planning. As stated earlier, operations planning provides detail about what services are offered, what outputs are planned and what outcomes are expected for the dollars expended. Performance/progress measurement is included as a basis for quarterly or annual reviews. Keep in mind that operations plans are *mission-driven*; strategic plans are *issue-driven*. Most confusion comes from the fact that both have goals and objectives, strategies, actions and performance metrics. For strategic thinkers, the key is to remember that your *strategic plan* should *only* deal with major issues and challenges that are impacting or will impact the community or a specific group of stakeholders. You are addressing those identified issues with a strategic plan that expresses *how* you plan to overcome them.

Whether termed issues, challenges or problems, this element of your plan in many ways defines *why* the agency or work team exists and describes some of its primary concerns. It will also contain issues/challenges related to internal operating efficiencies or effectiveness that influence performance, productivity and cost. When crafting issues and challenges for a work team or larger unit, first consider the Mission, and why the organization is there in the first place. Many plans have issues totally unrelated to the Mission, which confuses the reader and weakens the plan. *Goals, objectives and strategies/actions all flow from the issues.* If there are no issues or problems, there will be very few, if any, goals or objectives, and no need for actions to address them.

Key Point: *Public agencies must create strategic plans to review and address the major issues and challenges the agency or community is facing. They are not written to express how the agency will manage its day-to-day operations. When developing a strategic plan, focus on existing or probable events or circumstances that must be addressed to protect people, prevent negative outcomes, preserve quality or develop the community. Public officials, administrators and agency managers must use their strategic plans to devote attention to highly important issues that have significant potential to damage, disrupt or inhibit quality of life for all or any element of the community.*

In sum, the ability to identify, analyze and articulate critical issues and challenges is the true genesis of your strategic plan. If you understand the issues and have good data, you can make a strong case for assigning funding priority. Issues having the greatest probability for introducing serious negative impact or damage to the community tend to get funded first.

Two Dimensions

I recommend the simple model in Figure 2 when beginning to identify issues and challenges. It emphasizes both the *external* and *internal* dimensions but also encourages staff to look at *both tangible* and *intangibles*. By this, I mean that the tendency is to focus on the tangible aspects of work, while neglecting the intangible. Both are critical, but the *intangibles* have the greatest ability to harm entire organizations and communities. It is human nature to deal with tangible problems and leave the more emotional and difficult 'people issues' alone. Proper strategic thinking and planning requires that all four dimensions be considered when identifying issues and challenges. Only by doing this will goals and objectives deal with important challenges being encountered by the community, agency or work team.

Summarizing, for public plans, issues and challenges *must* be identified in two primary dimensions, *external* and *internal*, and address secondary dimensions dealing with *tangible* and *intangible* issues. Keep in mind that external issues are those residing in the broader community, or are outside your agency. This includes internal support organizations that serve other departments and perhaps not the general public. Internal issues are those occurring *inside* government, in virtually every government organization. Identifying them is essential for continuous improvement efforts because they create the underpinning for improvement planning. Far too many organizations ignore this planning element due to an inherent fear of showcasing internal problems and because it is easier and safer to focus on external, issue-driven problems in the community. As you begin planning, keep the following diagram in mind.

New Strategic Thinking

Issue Category Identification

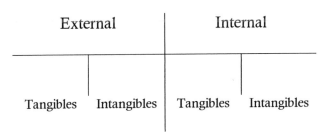

External   Internal

Tangibles   Intangibles   Tangibles   Intangibles

Figure 2.

Tangibles and Intangibles

Human nature tends to skew both the planning process and its desired outcomes. In planning and execution, people naturally focus on tangible issues and shy away from those tending to be less finite. In work sessions, if you do not direct discussion in a manner that differentiates issues and challenges that are easily documented or assessed from those that are more feeling, opinion, or culture-related, participants will spend most of their effort on tangibles. For example, when you begin identifying *internal* issues, the list will include everything from location to funding, décor, equipment, staffing, and the inadequacy of storage facilities. You will rarely get deep and meaningful discussions about a dysfunctional culture unless it is a planned, facilitated review. This is far different than informal gripe sessions about people, process, management, errant behavior or morale.

Similarly, in work sessions dedicated to *external* issues there will be ample review of issues associated with water systems, roads, wastewater, solid waste, park facilities, recreational opportunities, crime rates, public education, zoning, ordinances, health status, immunization rates, the number of homeless, and many other visible, countable and assessable problems throughout the state or municipality. Rarely will there be meaningful discussions about image, trust, and community relations unless the facilitator creates that opportunity.

More examples will be provided in the following sections that discuss internal and external issues. The takeaway is that human nature and group dynamics often exclude subjects that are more difficult to assess and that create natural polarity. Yet, intangibles are often the most detrimental forces in a government, agency or community.

Understanding Internal Issues

Internal issues are those existing within the organization that affect efficiency, quality, productivity, harmony or overall effectiveness. In many ways, they are forces that inhibit performance or keep the organization from accomplishing its mission. Lack of training, loss of expertise due to retirements, lack of operating space, insufficient computing power, poor or worn-out equipment, or an insufficient number of employees to accomplish the mission are all examples of internal issues. During early-stage planning discussions, issues such as these are often identified by managers and employees, yet by themselves are not directly related to the mission. However, they could very well determine the agency's ability to effectively conduct its work. As planning activities begin, you will find that most employees are more willing to identify *internal* issues before gravitating to external, more mission-related issues. This is because they confront internal issues every day and are sensitive to how they inhibit their ability to accomplish daily tasks.

Examples of Internal Issues

In a group setting, I typically ask, 'What are the most significant internal *tangible* issues that impact/inhibit your ability to do your work or accomplish your mission?' The range of responses is large and always interesting. Below are examples of typical responses. Notice how they fall into particular categories.

- There is insufficient staff to accomplish our mission.

- Patrol vehicles have an average of 205,000 miles on them and are constantly breaking down.

- Training has been reduced to the point that very few current employees are able to keep pace with the new systems and processes being installed.

- Due to budget shortfalls and subsequent layoffs, we have not replaced four trucks and five graders that were decommissioned last year and are now late on 5 out of 10 maintenance projects. (*an internal issue with an external impact.*)

- Records storage remains primarily hard copy when the world has moved to more cost effective electronic storage; the City has insufficient hard copy storage space for its current and projected archived files.

- The Legislature does not understand the value of our services and has continued to ignore efforts to increase the budget to meet citizen-driven program demands.

- There has been a 175% increase in the number of requests for the City's summer recreational programs but there are not enough facilities to accommodate this level of service.

- City expansion has outpaced growth of fire stations, which has extended response times, increased insurance rates, and inhibited the ability to safely serve the growing community.

- Court cases have increased by 127% in just three years, yet the number of officers and court employees has been reduced by seven FTEs. This has balooned case load, increased overtime costs, slowed processing, and created a huge case backlog.

I frequently see issue categories that reflect concerns about staffing, training/expertise, equipment, facilities, morale, politics, lack of understanding and support, and the big one – insufficient funding. The issue of funding will only get more severe. Its implications will be far reaching and long-term.

As you begin planning sessions, assuming there has first been comprehensive training on strategic planning and the planning process, I encourage you to begin with group sessions conducted to identify internal issues. Employees become more engaged and are generally prone to spirited discussion because internal issues become quite personal. Administrative professionals can demonstrate significant emotion over dated software, lack of space, slow computers, antiquated CRTs, and obsolete policies. Quality, along with efficient and effective work is hampered by these types of tangible issues and all inhibit the ability to achieve the mission. The same is true for any public agency. Tangible internal issues are frequent discussion topics for police, courts, fire, wastewater treatment, solid waste, water, health, transportation, road maintenance, parks, education, corrections, and every other facet of state and local government. Asking a planning group to identify internal tangible issues can open a floodgate of knowledge...and frustration.

Some of the more common topical tangible issue 'buckets' or categories are:

- Funding

- Staff levels (insufficient staff)

- Compensation levels

- Capability of existing employees (loss of knowledge and skill through retirement, layoffs, or people leaving to seek other opportunities)

- Office/computing equipment and software

- Facilities and furnishings

- Supplies

- Organization structure

- Statutes, ordinances and policy framework (outdated, misused, misconstrued, inappropriate)

- Capital equipment and vehicles

- Employee development and training

- Career options

Keep in mind that employees don't raise 'issues' that are positive and laudatory. If you ask them to identify the issues and problems that inhibit their ability to conduct efficient and effective work, you will get just that —a list of problems and frustrations. Be an active listener. Don't worry about all the 'negative' things you hear—these are descriptions of real problems. Record comments and make certain all participants know they are being heard and face no penalty for their candor. If this initial process begins well, reviewing external issues will be even more productive.

In sum, in government, while many citizens have the erroneous perception that government offices are flush with ample money, space, staff, training and equipment, the opposite is actually true. For the output expected, many state and local government agencies have too few people, inadequate or insufficient equipment, marginal facilities, and funding that is insufficient to accomplish various missions. Certainly, many state and local government agencies are amply staffed and equipped, but without sustained funding levels that accompany population growth, they, too, will see steady decline. All of the above have become standard categories identified by state and local governments I have visited. There is enormous value in work sessions that allow managers and employees to identify internal tangible issues that negatively impact their ability to perform. Even if senior administrators and managers are confident they can identify the issues without employee input, involving employees is still crucial. After all, they are the ones who will have to implement the solutions.

Internal Intangibles

Involving employees is even more important when identifying *intangible* internal issues. However, intangibles generate much more emotional discussion and must be carefully facilitated. While some participants are quite willing to air frustrations, others will be reluctant. Identifying internal intangible issues and challenges takes an experienced group leader who can create and sustain a trusting environment that promotes honesty without generating finger-pointing, accusations, blaming, and emotional tirades. For this reason, in my experience, most managers avoid discussions about intangibles because they are related to interactions among people and overall group dynamics. Many do not have the training or personality traits necessary to lead group discussions involving frustrations within the group or between and among agencies. However, through our management, leadership and organizational studies, it is clear that over 70% of issues in public organizations are intangible. And, as any experienced manager knows, people issues are among the most debilitating to overall productivity.

Some will be wondering what I am talking about and why I am taking time in a discussion about strategic planning to review internal intangible issues. Very simply, it is because a significant number of issues related to productivity, quality, efficiency, and organization effectiveness can be traced directly to issues involving communication, cooperation, and collaboration. Among the most frequently identified intangible internal issues are:

- Poor communication
- Poor cooperation
- Lack of collaboration (typically a combination of the previous two)
- Negative political environment
- Lack of acknowledgement or appreciation
- An uncaring environment
- Low morale

- Instability
- Lack of loyalty
- Lack of trust
- Poor leadership (perceived)
- Insufficient listening

As you review the list, can you imagine a work environment with these types of issues? Would it be healthy, productive, efficient, harmonious, or resilient? Could it possibly be less effective than it would be if these issues were addressed? Avoiding discussions about intangible internal issues is foolish. These are the issues that can limit productivity, sink a career or hamper your ability to achieve program missions. Take time to identify intangibles that inhibit your organization. It takes courage, but the payoff can be huge.

Understanding External Issues

External issues are the problems or negative situations existing in the community that relate to a particular mission. In other words, a Bureau of Highway Safety should focus on problems associated with accidents and unsafe conditions on state roadways. In this instance, the best expression of an issue, problem or challenge is statistical information related to the number of incidents, deaths and injuries occurring on roads and highways over a set period of time.

A County Assessor will focus on issues related to growth in service demand, local economics, property values, internal efficiency, customer complaints, etc. Public health officials will address issues and challenges that deal with the most critical areas of the community's health, such as immunization levels, food, water and air quality, infectious disease prevalence, etc. Parks and Recreation will deal with the condition of facilities and equipment, service demand, location, acquiring adequate facilities, etc. And Public Works will identify issues relating to traffic congestion, road conditions, infrastructure deterioration, growing service demands, equipment serviceability, etc. Every agency and each element within an agency will have specific external issues and challenges that relate to its Mission. Some will overlap, which is helpful because this tends to showcase the most critical problems having broad community impact. Highway Safety and the State Transportation Department have many of the same issues as the State Highway Patrol. However, with different missions and capabilities, they will (cooperatively, we hope) address the issues through different strategies and actions.

External issues are found outside the agency and are those problems or conditions the agency is there to address. The list below provides examples of agency types with typical issue categories. There are many more for each organization. Hopefully, these samples will help clarify the nature of external issues.

Law Enforcement – issues related to crime, homeland security, public safety, etc.

Water Utility – issues related to water purity, supply, demand cycles, system security, system failures, etc.

Solid Waste – issues related to landfill capacity, location, hazardous waste disposal, growing demand, etc.

Public Health – issues related to food safety, drinking water safety, nutrition, immunization levels, disease outbreaks, STDs, health education, etc.

Public Works – issues related to road surface quality, drainage problems, watershed capacity, emergency response, water and wastewater systems, wastewater capacity, wastewater demand, etc.

Education – issues related to annual yearly progress, population growth, classroom size, facility maintenance, student demopraphics and student needs, nutrition, transportation, etc.

Planning and Zoning – issues related to population growth, annexation, new service requirements, fire and police coverage, economic impact, etc.

Fire Departments – issues related to population growth, response times, homeland security, coverage, jurisdictional coordination, etc.

Libraries – issues related to growing service demands (or reduced demand due to Internet usage, computers, television), material costs, theft of materials, loss of public support, poor location to serve citizens, etc.

This is not an exhaustive list. There are many, many agencies, Commissions, Boards and programs; all have external issues—even those that serve other public agencies.

Every public agency can identify external issues it is or will be addressing. Some administrative support agencies (such as information technology or purchasing) deal with public organizations so their external issues will typically be with another department or element of government. The preceding list is illustrative only. There are dozens of state and local public agencies that are not on this list but ALL have and are addressing external issues and challenges. Public transportation, courts, Prosecuting and City Attorneys, schools, environmental quality, economic development, planning, building departments, Assessors, Clerks, Coroners, Treasurers, and many other public organizations could be used as examples.

The external dimension deals with the world outside the agency or organization. It deals with the community and with the issues that relate directly to the Mission. The internal dimension focuses on the organization itself and issues or problems that influence its productivity, harmony, efficiency or effectiveness.

Summary

In each of these primary dimensions, it is essential to identify both tangible *and* intangible issues. Tangible issues generally concern people, facilities, equipment, funding, and anything that can be counted, inventoried, bought, sold, procured or repaired. Intangibles, on the other hand, are the most neglected area of planning because they deal with issues or problems related to morale, attitude, trust, loyalty, public opinion, image, communication, cooperation, collaboration, leadership, commitment, initiative, creativity, and overall culture. This is an avoided area of planning in both private and public sectors because very few people know how to deal with it effectively. People therefore tend to focus on the areas they can touch, count, and feel, ignoring those that cause the most harm to the organization.

Much of this book is dedicated to leaving legacies that build learning, cooperative and harmonious organizations that openly review and learn from *both* internal and external intangible issues. It takes courage to review internal and external intangibles, but to refrain from doing so will predispose the organization to continual problems and potential failure.

Internal issues are those occurring inside government—in every government organization. Identifying them is essential for continuous improvement efforts because they create the underpinning for improvement planning. Far too many organizations ignore this planning element due to an inherent fear of showcasing internal problems and because it is easier and safer to focus on external, mission-driven problems in the community.

An Inclusive Process

I cannot over-emphasize that the process of issue identification is the best place to involve employees and develop a culture that focuses on continuous improvement. You cannot improve if you are unwilling or unable to identify issues or problems that need to be addressed and state them clearly. Get people involved with identifying issues related to the organization's central purpose. If you are in law enforcement, you must identify issues related to crime and public safety; if you are in public health, take time to identify all the issues related to community health (immunization rates, water sanitation, restaurant food safety, environmental health, etc.); if you are a public works agency, identify issues associated with roads, signage, bridges, drainage, maintenance, traffic, etc. The same is true for libraries, schools, environmental protection, planning and zoning, public transportation, building, facilities management, Clerks, Treasurers, IT departments, and every other possible facet of state and local government. Regardless of your agency's role, it is there for a reason and must address various internal and external issues. What are they?

Employees at all levels see problems first-hand and enjoy being involved with this aspect of planning. Of all the activities related to strategic planning, this is the area that attracts people and gets them engaged. Building a habit of inclusion and participation should be one of the most enduring aspects of the planning legacy.

Writing Proper Issue Statements

There is a tendency to state an issue or problem as a solution, or to state it in such general terms that it has no value. To write, 'The number of highway deaths and serious injuries is too high and must be reduced' is weak and virtually meaningless. *An issue or problem statement must be stated in terms that 1) Concisely describes the issue or problem, and 2) Explains the ramifications and conveys the relevance of the situation.*

Two of the most important words in planning:

So What?

Remember these words! Any issue (a problem statement) that does *not* have inherent clarity about its importance or impact *must* be written in a manner that communicates *why* the issue is relevant. Statistics are often powerful enough to reflect the ramification or seriousness of the issue without additional words to answer, '*So what?*'

Example #1:

> In the past fiscal year, 42 children were seriously injured or killed on the state's highways while not wearing safety belts— a 37% increase in just three years.

Example #2:

> There was an 86% increase in the number of school days lost from 2009 to 2010 due to illness from preventable childhood disease. Immunization rates for preventable childhood disease stand at 59%, down from 82% in 2004, and over 20% below the CDC's minimum recommended levels.

Example #3:

> Fully 35% of all water mains in the city's water system are
> over 60 years old; the average life span approximates 40 years
> and the number of serious breaks has increased from 4 per
> year to an average of 15 per year over the past three years,
> costing the City an average of $1,450,500 annually in
> unfunded emergency repairs.

Example #4:

> There are currently 211 bridges in the state that do not
> comply with existing safety and construction codes. This has
> increased the probability of a serious public safety threat, has
> jeopardized federal funding and may increase the state's
> exposure to liability.

None of the first three examples needs a lot of additional information to
express the issue or problem. Just reading them provides a feeling of
seriousness and impact. For organizations that have reasonably good
statistical data, it is always advisable to use it to showcase the most
pressing issues, problems and/or challenges the agency or community is
facing. Example #4 uses statistics for clarity but has included potential
ramifications to answer the question, *"So what?"* Merely reciting statistics
may not sufficiently explain why the issue or problem is important.
Adding an explanation will both increase its value and educate the
reader, which typically makes a difference when it comes to budget
allocation or public support. It is very important to *not* add extraneous
detail or editorial comment. The statement must be short, clear, concise
and powerfully written. While there is a tendency to editorialize in an
issue or problem statement, it is much more powerful if short and
concise. The rule is,

*IF there are statistics that clearly and powerfully reveal the issue or
problem, use them and let them stand alone. If the problem can be
reflected by using a combination of explanatory text and numbers but
does not answer the question, 'So what?' add a brief one or two sentence
statement that explains predictable or inevitable negative outcomes.*

What about the elements of the organization that do not provide wholly visible external services to the community? There are many departments, divisions, bureaus or sections that provide general services that may be administrative in nature—human resources, purchasing, legal, risk management, information services, facility maintenance, finance, budget office, Clerk, Treasurer, courts, etc. Are issues and challenges just as relevant here? Absolutely! It merely requires a different way of looking at the operation to determine existing issues and challenges. What causes the most heartburn? What frustrates staff or clients? Is the operation as efficient and effective as it can possibly be? Is demand growing? Is there good public support or a negative image? These questions indicate several issue categories that can be explored.

Merely reciting statistics may not clearly explain why the issue or problem is important. Adding an explanation will both increase its value and educate the reader, which might make a big difference when it comes to budget allocation or public support.

Remember, an issue or problem can be *internal* or *external*, *tangible* or *intangible*. Is the office as collaborative and harmonious as you would like? What evidence is there that it is highly efficient? Is the work backlog growing? Are public complaints escalating? Are systems declining?

Data is everywhere. Yet, I am consistently amazed by the number of people who complain that they have insufficient statistical information about their operation. When I begin asking questions about the organization, there are always issues that cause great frustration, such as the number of telephone calls that interrupt their workflow. All right, but how many calls come in? How often? What is the average length? How large is the backlog? How many minutes, hours or days does it take to respond to service requests? What is the cost per transaction? All of these are countable, can be analyzed, and will provide the basis for stating an issue or problem. Even for those public organizations that do not traditionally keep formal data, it is all around them. Once the team gets into the habit of identifying issues, it can be guided into the practice of generating data to illuminate the problem and to track and measure the remediation process. In fact, I often suggest that data gathering be listed as a strategy or action in the strategic plan.

Properly Written Issues

The ability to properly state issues and challenges becomes both skill and art. Those who can successfully explain issues are often those who retain existing funds or generate new funding. Keep in mind that public programs and services are in place to address issues. They do not exist merely to spend tax money. So, the better you can express issues, the better the public and decision-makers can understand why you exist and what you are trying to accomplish.

Also keep in mind that issue statements are problem statements. They must clearly state the problem and its actual or potential impact on the community or constituent group. I cannot overemphasize that issue statements should not be written as solutions. This is the Achilles Heel of so many plans. Far too many plan writers tend to state the solution instead of expressing the problem in clear, powerful terms.

The following are properly crafted issue statements that have the essential elements—a clearly stated problem with appropriate data, along with a review of the actual or potential impact. Keep in mind that, unless the data is potent enough to convey impact, you need to express what the impact will most likely be if the issue/problem is not addressed.

Example #1: City Police Department

> A major type of reported criminal offenses is personal property crime and includes theft, vandalism and burglary. In 2010, there were a combined total of 1,429 property-type crimes, almost 70% of all reported offenses. This is a 57% increase in property crime in the past three years. Such growth has increased case backlog by over 30%, reduced resources available for patrol and investigation, increased overtime costs, reduced time spent on each case, impacted case solvability and property recovery, and has created image problems for the City—a potential negative for economic development.

Example #2: City Fire Department

Based on even the lowest recommended service levels in local jurisdictions, there are not enough fire stations to deploy adequate personnel and equipment during emergencies and maintain sufficient backup required by fire safety standards. This compounds the City's liability in emergency situations, jeopardizes emergency personnel, and places citizens and property at avoidable risk. Simultaneous calls for even basic services immediately overtax the current system, potentially leading to a serious situation given two or more emergency calls. (One residential fire call immediately overtaxes the current system, exceeding OSHA and NFPA guidelines and adding to the City's legal liability and exposure.)

Example #3 County Recreation Department

Requests for indoor recreational programs have increased by 237% in four years. Summer program participation has grown from 4,816 to 11,730 in five years and the waiting list for new programs exceeds staffing or facilities to accommodate recreational needs or growing sport team demand. Due to insufficient staff, accidents have also increased from 29 in 2007 to 177 in 2010, placing the County in jeopardy for expensive tort claims. Overall program growth mirrors public expectations/demand, but there are insufficient funds for staff and facilities, which has resulted in public outcry, more at-risk young people on the streets, escalating liability, and reduced quality of life for residents.

Example #4: Public Transportation

Public Transportation's basic operating costs (particularly fuel, insurance and operator salary/benefits) continue to increase at rates greater than fare box revenues, resulting in the need to increase revenues (via fare increases) or reduce operating costs by reducing services. From 2005 to 2010, fuel costs grew from $409,838 annually to $1,188,324 in 2010; insurance has grown from $167,405 in 2005 to $249,297 in

2010. Over the same period, personnel operating costs grew from $5,030,085 annually to $6,693,736. Overall, operating costs have grown 41% since 2005. Insufficient funding has reduced the ability to meet growing demand (up 130% since 2005), limits public mobility, drastically affects those with special needs and the disadvantaged, and slows the City's economic development program.

Example #5: Street Maintenance

The City's Snow Plan currently enables the Division to accomplish plowing and spreading material on Emergency Snow Routes (560 lane-miles), the remaining arterials, and bus routes (556 lane-miles) within a 10 to 14 hour timeframe. During heavy snowfall, this timeframe does not match public expectations due to an insufficient amount of dedicated snow removal equipment and staff. This is a periodic issue, but when it occurs, it can quickly reach crisis, creating public outcry and anger among local businesses and residents, impacting business vitality and adding risk to citizens.

Example #6: Administration – Water Utilities

Erroneous radio reads from water meters (575 out of 462,433 billings) for an average cost of $804.23 per error, continue to create billing adjustments, increase costs, reduce efficiency, lower productivity, and loss of Department credibility. Great progress was made during the past year, but the Customer Service Section anticipates ongoing issues with meters that were programmed by personnel prior to receiving proper training or with meters that have defective radio read equipment. These factors increase the number of customer contacts (it takes an average of 2 hours staff time per adjustment), increase backlog, facilitate errors, and limit the ability to provide quality financial data.

Example #7: City Attorney

In 2010 the City Attorney's Criminal Division opened 1,235 *more* misdemeanor cases than in the previous year—a 27% increase. The Division also opened 1,681 *more* traffic cases than in the previous year—a 26% increase. Growth in caseload with no corresponding increase in staff, equipment or facilities has increased backlog, reduced the time attorneys spend on each case, increased overtime costs and slowed the judicial process. There have been increasing morale issues and frustrations that have resulted in the highest turnover rate in the state.

Example #8: Public Works

The City has approximately 1,800 miles of sidewalk, much of which, due to various issues like utility settlements, tree roots, etc., is deteriorating and does not meet A.D.A. standards. As a result, the City will continue to face several hundred citizen complaints each year, a growing number of injury claims against the City due to people tripping and falling, and more complaints specifically related to A.D.A. non-compliance. This will result in major fines and legal settlements against the City, costing millions of dollars. The conservative cost estimate to bring the entire sidewalk network into A.D.A. compliance is $60 million. Since the City has not remained current on sidewalk maintenance, it will be difficult to get and remain current unless existing defects can be addressed in a short time period. The allocation for sidewalk repair has been inconsistent and well below what would allow for more timely completion of repair to bring all walks up to standard. An allocation of $4 million/year would allow the City to begin reducing the $60 million deficit and help reduce liability risk, as well as stay compliant with federal regulations to ensure continued receipt of federal funds by all city agencies. The allocation for sidewalk repair is $750,000 for the current budget year.

Example #9: State Health Department

> Childhood immunization rates have fallen from 83% to <60% since 2005, while the number of reported cases of school days lost due to mumps, measles, and whooping cough have increased by 312% statewide. The CDC recommends a minimum of 80% immunization rates to avoid epidemics among school-age children. Higher disease levels have increased medical costs for families, increased health risks associated with childhood diseases, jeopardized federal funding, and created a difficult teaching/learning environment due to large numbers of absent students.

As you read the above examples, notice that the issues neither include a lot of ancillary explanation of *why* this has occurred nor provide solutions. This is a critical point. Issue statements should *never* include a 'story line.' They provide enough basic data and associated facts to express the problem; then they answer the question, 'So what?' by providing insight regarding anticipated impact. They are not intended to tell a long story and do not include editorials about what should be done to address the issue; that is done through strategies and actions.

Once your team gets into the habit of identifying issues, you can develop the practice of generating data to illuminate the problem and to track and measure the remediation process. In fact, I often suggest that data gathering be listed as a strategy or action item in the plan.

Remember the audience. Most strategic plan readers do not fully understand your world, whether you work for a Clerk or Treasurer's Office, library, a school, utility, public works, police, or fire department, the court system, etc. This is your world. Therefore, your issue statements must use good data, be clearly written and express impact. As emphasized in Part I of this book, if a highly probable or predicted event occurs but has little or no impact, the public chorus will be a resounding, 'So what?' You are strategic thinkers who are professional subject matter experts. It is your responsibility to report truth and supply adequate data to support the reported issues and challenges.

Once an elected official or any form of final decision-maker (or the general public) knows the truth, the decision is theirs. It may not be the decision you want or believe is in the best interest of your constituents or the community, but you have done your professional best to express the facts and the possible/predictable outcomes. I often tell elected officials that, once they know the facts, it is their decision and they can '*Choose your news*' depending on that reality. Unfortunately, in tough times, this is a very difficult proposition, and it will not become easier in the decades ahead.

Issue Identification – An Eight-Step Process

Convening staff to discuss issues is one of the most energizing facets of strategic plan development. External issues are known and understood by employees and they very quickly get into the exercise. The same is true for internal issues. Employees live every day with internal issues and challenges and, with little coaxing and coaching, will begin identifying those that frustrate their ability to achieve their mission, reduce efficiency, hamper productivity, or hurt morale. Good facilitation is important. Knowing the right questions is essential. Done well, this part of the process generates great information, provides enormous insight, and brings the team together like no other exercise.

As you begin issue identification, consider the following eight steps:

1. Each manager should convene a strategic planning team or representatives from a specific work unit that has a distinct mission. It might be a small department, Commission, division, bureau, section, or even smaller unit of a large department. *Key:* The group deals with a specific mission. If you have a small agency, consolidation of this process is possible, especially if you have one collective mission.

2. Begin with external tangible issues/challenges, asking, 'What are the most significant *tangible* issue and challenge *categories* this group is currently facing or will face in the near future? *Key:* Don't identify specific issues at this point—just the categories. For example, if you are a law enforcement agency, focus initially

on the *categories* of issues you face, such as vehicle traffic, gangs, drugs, personal property crime, community policing, etc.

3. Next, for each identified category, take time to identify the specific issues the unit is encountering or will face in the next year or so. For instance, continuing with the law enforcement example, what are the issues related to vehicle traffic you must contend with? What are the specific issues related to drug usage and trafficking in the community? Brainstorm issues for each category—but limit discussion and don't try to fully explain at this point.

4. After you have listed key external tangible categories and under each have listed in a sentence or two what the specific issues are, move to *external intangible* issues. What are the intangible issues that impact the unit? Consider public image, trust, interagency collaboration, cooperation, and communication, community support, media support, etc. I suggest doing this step in the same meeting as Step 3.

5. In a separate meeting that may include the same group but can also involve other employees, identify the major *internal tangible* issues and challenges that impact your ability to fulfill the mission. What tangible factors inhibit the work unit? Typically, employees will identify space, policies, staff levels (FTEs), funding, equipment, salaries, etc. Move fast and try to refrain from too much venting. Just get the facts down and gain agreement that these factors are internal tangible issues that affect *productivity*, *efficiency*, *effectiveness*, *quality* or *cost*.

6. In another session, identify the major *internal intangible* issues and challenges that impact the ability to achieve your mission or impact productivity, efficiency, effectiveness, quality or cost. Typical internal intangibles are morale, loyalty, communication, collaboration, cooperation, communication, acknowledgement, appreciation, recognition, flexibility, etc.

Note: For internal issues and challenges in larger organizations it is often helpful to conduct employee surveys to avoid the vent-fest that can accompany discussions of internal tangible and intangible issues. People want to be heard and appreciate the opportunity to share their thoughts. But, it can burn a lot of time and generate negatives if not handled properly. Done well, surveys will provide the required information. However, if facilitated properly, a team always benefits from a process of identifying internal issues and challenges.

7. After each group session, assign or seek volunteers who are subject matter experts (SMEs) to develop each identified issue into a strong statement with appropriate data and explanation. All writers should have received training in how to properly articulate issue statements so they can insert adequate data and answer the inherent question, 'So what?' Provide several days to craft issue statements and return to a central compiler. *This is the critical step;* writers must be able to dedicate the time and have the capacity to write powerful and accurate issue statements. Remember, issues provide the foundation for goals and objectives. Good issues are the basis for potent, meaningful strategic plans.

8. Once all internal and external issues are prepared (tangibles and intangibles) and compiled, share with the planning team or selected employee representatives to ensure they properly capture and express the issue. Amend as required, then prioritize and decide which ones are significant enough to be included in the strategic plan. Remember that public sector strategic plans are *issue-driven* and are *not* operations plans. It is ultimately a management decision as to which issues are included in the strategic plan, representing the most salient issues the agency wishes to share with elected officials, stakeholders and the public. Once the final selection is made, prepare to develop goals and objectives associated with each major issue.

Note: Internal issues and challenges may not be selected for inclusion in the published strategic plan because many, such as 'low wages or insufficient funding' can seem self-serving and others, such as issues with cooperation, location, poor equipment, etc., may not be true strategic issues. However, do not lose the identified issues. These will be placed in the agency's Internal Improvement or Operations Plans. Some issues remain important even if not truly strategic; they can be addressed in other elements of your organization's executive planning process.

Facilitation is Critical

Anyone who has invested time in issue identification will understand the value of good facilitation. In addition to training in strategic plan development, it is important to have training in group dynamics or group facilitation before trying to facilitate work sessions where internal and external issues are being identified. From my experience, it is important to focus on each issue category and address them one at a time. In larger organizations, surveys can be used to gather employee input on internal issues backed by focus groups that can verify assembled data. Whether you hire a facilitator or use internal talent, communicate your intent early, clearly and often, and make it an inclusive process. Tangible external issues are easy; they are the issues professionals grapple with every day and that keep them awake at night. For those, the challenge is articulation. A good facilitator will take time to generate enough information that can showcase each issue in a manner that is accurate, powerful and meaningful to the community. After this is accomplished, it is merely a matter of developing each issue in final draft form.

Summary – Issues and Challenges

The basis for public sector strategic planning is the list of the most critical issues and challenges the department, agency or community is facing. Well-written issues share important data and informed interpretation of predicted internal and external outcomes that the program, section, bureau, division, or agency is, or will be, encountering. Plans provide the basis for budgets; issues are the driving force behind plans.

Keep the following in mind:

- Good issues provide foundation and rationale for goals, objectives, strategies and actions.

- Issues are adaptive – they change as the community evolves, as the agency adapts, as client needs evolve, as new legislation emerges and as new challenges emerge. Issues are the *problems* and *needs* that define why you're there.

- Issues are *not* solutions and are not written as such.

- Good issue statements are potent problem statements that provide direction and clarity of purpose for organizational programs; they provide rationale for budget requests and, in many ways, justify why the agency or program exists.

- Issues are problem/challenge statements that must be written to state the *problem* and the *ramifications/impact* of the problem; if there is no impact, no answer to the critical question, 'So what?,' there will be little support for the issue. This is an essential element of this contemporary and unique public planning process. If a program or agency cannot produce meaningful issues that have significant impact, there is some likelihood that program or agency is no longer needed or is less valuable than in the past. It might also signify that is has done a great job and has been highly successful at solving problems and fulfilling its intended mission.

Chapter 14

Constructing Accurate Goals and Measurable Objectives

Once there are properly written issue statements, constructing goals and objectives is relatively simple. This is especially true if good data is included in the issue from which there can be a determination whether the value is too high, too low or meets expected standards. Without data this is very difficult. This chapter combines goals and objectives because they have similar origin and distinct similarities.

Over forty years ago, the RAND Corporation pioneered various styles of strategic planning and systems and provided training to the federal government. From all accounts, this training was excellent but very little consistently trickled down to state and local government. While there have been attempts to standardize process and language, it still appears that few state, county, city or town government strategic plans have properly written goals or objectives. As described previously, most are written as actions or strategies, then improperly labeled 'goals' or 'objectives.' This chapter will provide clear examples of this dilemma and demonstrate how errant goals and objectives can easily be corrected to become viable, measurable elements of your plan.

As you consider the rules below, recall the following diagram:

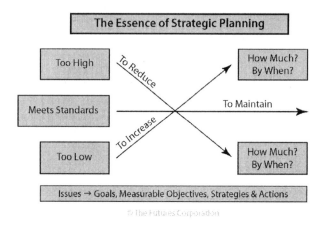

Figure 3.

I encourage you to consider everything in your work and within your professional purview. For the work you do each day, or for which you are responsible to the community, consider every possible issue in each category of public service. Without exception, you will be able to determine if the values associated with that topical area are within acceptable parameters or not. If they are not, they will either be unacceptably high or unacceptably low. As strategic thinkers, once you realize that public sector strategic plans address *only* major issues and challenges and *not* general operational planning, you will be able to focus your energies on clear goals and objectives that increase or reduce non-conforming values, or you will establish goals and objectives that maintain values that represent desired standards. This is the very essence of public strategic planning and the foundation for true goals and objectives.

Simple Rules:

1. Goals and objectives are typically not always presented alike in the public and private sectors. These two sectors have entirely different purposes in society.

2. Traditionally, goals and objectives typically begin with the word 'To.' This helps standardize presentation.

3. For public agencies, goals and objectives seek to increase, reduce (or decrease), or maintain a stated value. If you see any other word after the word '*To*,' I can pretty much guarantee that you are reading an action or strategy. A classic 'weasel word' is *improve*; to improve something is not a good goal.

4. When reviewing specific data that provides a value, the critical questions are, 'What is too high that must be reduced? What is too low that must be increased?' Or, 'What is within an established standard that you wish to (or must) maintain?' In the public sector, *every issue* (problem) or challenge can be distilled down into these three questions, which provide the basic foundation for what the strategic plan addresses as well as for its goals and objectives. This why identifying issues and assembling good data is absolutely critical before crafting goals and objectives.

5. Goals normally cover three to five years, but can extend twenty or more. Objectives are almost always annual or biannual and tell what will be accomplished (increased, reduced or maintained) during a specific budgeting period.

6. Goals are *inherently* quantifiable and do not normally contain numbers or percentages. The litmus test for a goal is, if I asked you in five years if you increased, reduced or maintained something stated in your plan, you should be able to tell me 'yes' or 'no.' If the goal is '*To increase immunization levels for all school age children*', or '*To reduce the number of deficient bridges that fall below current safety standards*,' the only relevant question in the future is "Did you or didn't you?" Objectives will

Goals provide direction toward general achievements or outcomes. Objectives provide specific, quantified and annual measured progress toward the same desired achievements or outcomes.

include a measurement expressing how much was achieved during a specified time period.

7. Objectives are *measurable* and are *time- specific* (usually one or two-year budget cycle). They should *always* use numbers for measurement and use percentages only if necessary. There will generally be one to several objectives for each goal, and they will *reflect measured progress toward the goal*. For the above goal example, an annual objective would be '*To increase, from 68% to at least 73%, the immunization levels for all school age children in the county, by (date).*' For the bridge goal, an objective would be '*To reduce, from 162 to <125 the number of substandard bridges statewide, by (date).*'

8. General strategies and specific actions would then tell *how* this will be accomplished; the budget reveals cost.

Questions abound regarding the differences between goals and objectives. Similar questions are raised about how actions or strategies relate to objectives. The following pages provide a variety of examples to help clarify the differences and demonstrate the relationships.

Problems arise from the human tendency to make every goal or objective an *activity*. Remember, a **goal** is *not* an action; it is a *result* or *outcome*. Think of it as a significant achievement that addresses all or part of an identified issue and relates to the original mission of the program involved. Once you have well-crafted issues, writing goals is fast and amazingly simple.

GOALS…Are like establishing a destination for which you must build a vehicle. This vehicle is comprised of more specific annual objectives, plus clear strategies and actions that will carry you toward the goal. Goals are **achievements**—*major accomplishments that define and represent desired quality outcomes. These quality outcomes in many ways also define your professional ideals and fundamental mission.*

Identifying and Selecting Goals

Goals do not appear from the ether. They are created from issue statements. Once issues are identified and properly written, goals become apparent. The only questions pertain to how many goals do you want to associate with any given issue and which are the most important to include in the strategic plan?

Goals do not just appear in a strategic plan without connection to an issue. As you review your current plan, if you find 'goals' that stand alone, they are most likely not goals but are restated elements of the mission or vision. They might be strategies or actions that have been mislabeled. Goals, on the other hand, are driven by issues. They cannot stand alone

Using some of the sample issue statements found in Chapter 14, it is simple to apply the model to ascertain goals.

Example #1: City Police Department

> A major type of reported criminal offense is personal property crime and includes theft, vandalism and burglary. In 2010, there were a combined total of 1,429 personal property type crimes, almost 70% of the total reported offenses. This is a 57% increase in property crime in the past three years. Such growth has increased case backlog by over 30%, reduced resources available for patrol and investigation, increased overtime costs, reduced time spent on each case, impacted case solvability and property recovery, and has created image problems for the City—a potential negative for economic development.

For Example #1, there are several options. If there is a belief that the number of personal property crimes is too high and can be reduced, the *primary goal* is *'To reduce the number of personal property crimes occurring in the city.'* Secondary goals, based on the reported impacts, might be: 1) To reduce the case backlog of personal property crimes; 2) To reduce total time and overtime associated with personal property crime; and 3) To reduce the total operating costs associated with personal property crimes.

There might also be a goal '*To reduce the amount of negative press being generated in the community that is associated with personal property crime.*'

The issue has foundational data and expresses effects associated with personal property crime. Because goals are to increase, reduce or maintain a standard, managers can review the issue, then easily identify goals.

Note: As with many issues involving escalating incidence or usage, a growing population might make reducing incidence difficult. In these cases, it is better to reduce incident growth rate or concentrate on reducing various impacts through innovative actions and strategies. In many cases, public managers know the numbers are going to increase, so must focus on modifying impact.

Example #2: County Recreation Department

> Requests for indoor recreational programs have increased by 237% in four years. Summer program participation has grown from 4,816 to 11,730 in five years, and the waiting list for new programs exceeds staffing or facilities to accommodate recreational needs or growing sport team demand. Due to insufficient staff, accidents have also increased from 29 to 177 since 2009, placing the County in jeopardy for expensive tort claims. Overall program growth mirrors public expectations/demand, but there are insufficient funds for staff and facilities, which has resulted in public outcry, more at-risk young people on the streets, escalating liability, and reduced quality of life for residents.

Example #2 can also be addressed several ways. If the population is growing and program requests will continue to increase, a goal to reduce the number of requests is impractical. As described above, managers will serve the community best by addressing impact. Several goals are apparent but two are especially important: 1) To reduce the number of accidents occurring among participants of County recreational programs; and 2) To reduce the number and cost of tort claims arising from injuries among county recreational programs. Because program requests will continue to stress resources and staff, the best goals will moderate impact.

Also, notice again that we are not expressing *how* the goal will be achieved. That is found in strategies and actions.

Example #3: Public Transportation

> Public Transportation's basic operating costs (particularly fuel, insurance and operator salary/benefits) continue to increase at rates greater than fare box revenues, resulting in the need to increase revenues (via fare increases) or reduce operating costs by reducing services. From 2005 to 2010, fuel costs grew from $409,838 annually to $1,188,324 in 2010; insurance has grown from $167,405 in 2005 to $249,297 in 2010. In the same period, personnel operating costs grew from $5,030,085 annually to $6,693,736. Overall, operating costs have grown 41% since 2005. Insufficient funding has reduced the ability to meet growing demand (up 130% since 2005), limits public mobility, drastically affects special needs and the disadvantaged, and slows the City's economic development program.

Because fuel costs cannot be controlled, goals and objectives will not address them. It is better to reduce the growth rate for operating costs. Many impacts listed for public transportation are endemic to the field. As costs grow and funding lags, it will be more difficult to meet growing demand, which will grow as socio-economic forces converge to reduce personal vehicle travel. As more city bus services are used, will funding increase or costs automatically decline? Of course not; that is why moderating operating costs is a reasonable goal.

Example #4: Administration – Water Utilities

> Erroneous radio reads from water meters (575 out of 462,433 billings) for an average cost of $804.23 per error (over $460,000 in additional cost), continue to create billing adjustments, increase costs, reduce efficiency, lower productivity, and loss of Department credibility. Great progress was made during the past year, but the Customer Service Section anticipates ongoing issues with meters that were programmed by personnel prior to receiving proper

training or with meters that have defective radio read equipment. These factors increase the number of customer contacts (it takes an average of 2 hours staff time per adjustment), increase backlog, facilitate errors, and limit the ability to provide quality financial data.

If, after reviewing the data and determining 575 erroneous meter reads per month is too high, at the very least a reasonable goal would be '*To reduce the number of erroneous meter reads,*' or '*To reduce the per error cost associated with erroneous reads.*'

Example #5: City Attorney

In 201,0 the City Attorney's Criminal Division opened 1,235 *more* misdemeanor cases than in the previous year—a 27% increase. The Division also opened 1,681 *more* traffic cases than in the previous year—a 26% increase. Growth in caseload with no corresponding increase in staff, equipment or facilities has increased backlog, reduced the time attorneys spend on each case, increased overtime costs and slowed the judicial process. There have been increasing morale issues and frustrations that have resulted in the highest turnover rate in the state.

The courts, city or county attorneys and Office of the Attorney General are all battling growing caseloads. A City Attorney does not have the power or means to reduce the number of traffic problems, reduce the number of citations, or improve driving quality, so there few options for goals or objectives. However, I would counsel the City Attorney to establish goals addressing backlog, overtime, and dedicated time per case.

It is clear that solutions involve more staff, equipment and innovative procedures but those are *strategies* and *actions*. Remember, you are setting a goal that tells what you plan to increase, reduce or maintain—a measurable value. '*To reduce the overall case backlog in the City Attorney's Office;*' '*To reduce the total amount of overtime dedicated to misdemeanor and traffic cases;*' and '*To reduce staff time allocated per case for all misdemeanor and traffic cases.*' As you read these three goals, understand that they beg the solution: funding and more FTEs; but those are solutions—not goals.

This is where managers must take time to consider *what* they can address, *not* how they plan to do so.

Example #6: Public Works

> The City has approximately 1,800 miles of sidewalk, much of which, due to various issues like utility settlements, tree roots, etc., is deteriorating and does not meet A.D.A. standards. As a result, the City will continue to face several hundred citizen complaints each year, a growing number of injury claims against the City due to people tripping and falling and more complaints specifically related to A.D.A. non-compliance. This will result in major fines and legal settlements against the City, costing millions of dollars. The conservative cost estimate to bring the entire sidewalk network into A.D.A. compliance is $60 million. Since the City has not remained current on sidewalk maintenance, it will be difficult to get and remain current unless existing defects can be addressed in a short time period. The allocation for sidewalk repair has been inconsistent and well below what would allow for more timely completion of repair to bring all walks up to standard. An allocation of $4 million/year would allow the City to begin reducing the $60-million deficit and help reduce liability risk, as well as stay compliant with federal regulations to ensure continued receipt of federal funds by all city agencies. The allocation for sidewalk repair is $750,000 for the current budget year.

Is it acceptable to have 1,800 miles of deteriorating and dangerous sidewalks that do not meet A.D.A. standards? If the answer is, 'No, this number is too high,' then the primary goal is simply, '*To reduce the miles of city sidewalk that pose health risks to citizens and do not meet A.D.A. standards.*' It is permissible to add more goals, such as, '*To reduce the number of incidents resulting in complaints, fines or settlements that hurt the City's image or add to its operating cost.*'

Note: The data provides clarity about what the goal needs to be. If a number is unacceptably high, such as too many miles of unsafe sidewalks, it is clear that the goal is to reduce that number. The annual objective will include a value expressing how much progress can be made in the coming fiscal year, given funding and support for planned actions.

Example #7: State Health Department

> Childhood immunization rates have fallen from 83% to <60% since 2005, while the number of reported cases of school days lost due to mumps, measles, and whooping cough have increased by 312% statewide. The CDC recommends a minimum of 80% immunization rates to avoid epidemics among school-age children. Higher disease levels have increased family medical costs, increased health risks associated with childhood diseases, jeopardized federal funding, and created a difficult teaching/learning environment due to large numbers of absent students.

This issue statement provides a classic foundation for goals and annual objectives. If it is determined that <60% is *too low*, the goal is simply, '*To increase immunization rates among the K–3 school population base.*' You can add additional goals, such as, '*To reduce the number of school days lost due to preventable childhood diseases*' or '*To reduce the number of school-based epidemics caused by low immunization rates in the K–3 population.*' All are important and all provide clarity about what you intend to accomplish. The goal never discusses *how* you intend to address the issue; it merely expresses *what* you intend to accomplish relative to the data provided in the issue statement.

Goals and Measurability

Very simply, goals are *inherently,* but not specifically, measurable. Taking any one of the goals provided in the examples, the key question to test *general* measurability is, '*Did you reduce/increase/maintain the...?*' The answer, based on data gathered over time, is *yes* or *no*. In the future, by reviewing the data, you will know if you did or didn't do what you said you would do. For elected officials and senior administrators, this is critical. For health department officials, properly written goals allow them to quickly ascertain progress by asking, '*Did you increase immunization rates?"* You either did or you didn't. And, the data will tell by how much.

Relating to an objective is easy, because a public sector objective is typically for one or two years and *provides an incremental progression toward established goals.* Objectives are discussed in the following section.

Good Goals, Bad Goals

I cannot over-emphasize that goals (and objectives) in government agencies must be written to increase, reduce or maintain an established value. Because it is human nature to think in action terms, when you review your plan, I wager that you will find many goals stated as strategies or activities. The following are *'goals'* taken from actual state and local government plans. I have removed language that would identify location or agency. Notice that most are activities and strategies; some are extensions of the mission, and others are meaningless editorial comments.

- To emphasize more completely the development of community resources.

- To build new collaborative relationships with local community voluntary agencies.

- To seek greater harmony and good will among community stakeholders.

- To construct 27 miles of new highway between ___ and ___.

- To complete lane striping and street markings for 16 lane-miles within the city limits.

- To foster greater communication with the City Council.

- To increase dialogue with library patrons to engender greater cooperation and investment in new facilities.

- To create and implement seven new mobile immunization clinics throughout the state over the next fiscal year.

- Develop a knowledgeable, proactive, and participatory public dedicated to maintaining the appropriate level of environmental quality.

- Integrate pollution prevention education and practices into public, private, and agency programs.

- Comply with applicable federal and state environmental legislation in a manner which is reasonable, flexible, cost-effective, and, to the extent permitted by law, appropriate to local conditions.

- Creating inter-agency cooperation is important and can magnify overall contribution to society. As such, it will be pursued with enthusiasm and a collaborative spirit.

- Establish partnerships with interested groups and citizens to address common environmental issues.

- Respond faster to water main breaks to reduce complaints and cost.

- To prepare stronger, more accurate analysis that will support decisions pertaining to deployment of corrections personnel.

- We believe in community service and as such will support through our efforts the programs and services offered by voluntary agencies and will collaborate to bring the best possible outcomes to all citizens.

- All district employees, students, parents and community members embrace the ___ school district's clearly articulated and communicated accountability standards.

- We place the highest value on student learning by delivering the district's curriculum.

- Use technology to maximize productivity and the rate and quality of student learning.

- Assure that statewide education operates as a seamless system without barriers between its various elements.

- Improve internal communications and cooperation with other agencies.

- Build a customer service ethic.

- Increase harmony within the department and among all county agencies.

- Construct the new fitness facility as part of the city's recreation program.

- Explore new methods of reducing overtime and stress associated with increased case loads.

All of the above were taken from existing plans, many of which are very attractive and nicely presented. As you read through the list, what was your reaction to various 'goals?' I have accumulated dozens of plans with hundreds of similar 'goals' and 'objectives.' Many are grammatically poor and very few are measurable, other than whether the agency undertook them or not. Most have no connection to an issue that is deemed strategically important to the agency, constituents or community. Some readers will argue that *doing* the actions indicated in many of the above will in fact accomplish something. That may be true, but these are not appropriate goals for public agencies.

By using *increase*, *reduce* or *maintain* you will establish a standard of presentation that connects to meaningful issues, relates to your mission and allows linear progression from issue to goal, objective, strategy and action. Strategies and actions are discussed in Chapter 15.

Goals are desired outcomes or achievements. They represent direction and quickly communicate your intent. If the data presents a value that is considered unacceptably high by professional staff or elected officials, the goal is to reduce that value. The same is true if the value is considered too low, such as immunization rates, landfill utilization, or recreational facility use; you will seek to increase that value. If you are meeting standards, such as those established for air and water quality, emergency response times, immunization rates, facility usage, caseload, etc. your goal would be '*To maintain.*' As you begin to identify goals, keep the following in mind:

- Goals are broad, longer-term, desired achievements and outcomes and are generally established for three to five years, or a decade or more. They establish a general framework and direction for your organization's programs, indicating what you intend to accomplish.

- When establishing goals, think 'over the horizon;' for some longer-term goals you might think about your organization's *legacy*—what it would like to achieve/accomplish.

- In virtually all decent planning tutorials, goals typically begin with the word 'To.' This maintains a clear format and standardizes presentation.

- Goals are *generally* quantifiable, meaning you can follow their progress and, if stated properly, can determine if a value was increased, reduced, or maintained. Specific numbers are not needed for goals.

- Goals are *not* numerous—6 to 12 per program, section, bureau, division, or agency may be sufficient, although some organizations choose to have many more.

- Remember that goals are absolutely *issue-driven*—they are derived from your issue statements. Mandates and legislation can also drive goals, but if analyzed, you will find that they also address issues.

Annual Objectives

Classic planning language and technique identifies a series of plan elements—issues (challenges or problems), goals, objectives, strategies and actions. Goals and objectives are very similar because both are driven by issues and indicate intended progress toward a desired value. Goals are longer-term; objectives are typically established for a one or two-year budget cycle. Some prefer to think of these two plan elements as long-term goals and short-term goals. I prefer the term 'objective' because the term differentiates it from a long-term goal and indicates intent to measure progress toward that short-term goal.

Many readers have received strategic planning training and understand the basic differences between goals and objectives. As with goals, for many planners the challenge is gaining more insight and greater skill in writing powerful, measurable objectives. For the most part, objectives:

- Are clear, quantifiable, measurable, and time specific.

- Typically begin with '*To...*'

- Are similar to goals, seeking to *increase*, *reduce* or *maintain* a value.

- Are shorter-term than goals; they can be quarterly, semi-annual, annual or biannual.

- Establish milestones toward longer-term goals and provide achievement benchmarks. They establish intended incremental progress toward a goal, which might take several years to achieve.

- Address a problem or issue and indicate planned measured achievement toward a desired outcome. They may also indicate the intent to maintain an established standard that is essential to the agency, constituents or community.

- Typically include specific measurement as part of the objective (numbers or percentages); objectives can be *outcomes* or *outputs*.

- Are not strategies or activities that explain *how* an issue is being addressed. They express *what* is to be achieved within the budget cycle. They are *planned, measured achievements* toward longer-term goals.

Again using a football metaphor, objectives are like the various yard markers on the field. If the goal is at the other end of the field, how far can you progress downfield toward that goal during this budget cycle? You might have only enough funding and staff resources to proceed thirty yards toward the goal, but that is measured progress. For each budget year, you will calculate measured progress toward the goal until it is achieved and the original issue no longer exists. Very possibly, once you have achieved the goal, you will change both goal and objective to 'maintain' if it then becomes an important performance standard. When reviewing properly constructed plans, you will see objectives with measurements indicating how a program or agency will:

- Reduce cost
- Increase the number of people served or services utilized
- Increase the level of safety, security, health, response, service
- Reduce cost per person or service/transaction
- Increase/reduce rates (numeric or percentage value)
- Reduce incidence, volume, or rates
- Reduce probability, frequency, or magnitude of impact
- Reduce time required to accomplish something
- Increase/reduce usage
- Reduce complaints (image)
- Maintain established standards

There are many more, but these provide some indication of how objectives can be prepared to indicate what you intend to accomplish toward a goal. If traffic congestion is too great and data indicate that wait time at traffic lights exceeds 4 minutes, this might be judged as too high. The goal

'To improve' is unacceptable. In my view, improve is a 'weasel word' that says nothing. It does not promote measurement because it neglects to inform whether the intent is to increase or reduce a measurable condition. And... **everything** *is measurable.*

would therefore be '*To reduce wait time...*' Your objective for the coming year could be '*To reduce, from 4 to < 3 minutes, the average wait time at downtown traffic lights.*' You may know the ideal is <2.5 minutes, but you do not have the resources to fully address the issue during the next year. So, you will employ several actions to reduce contributing factors as much as you feel is possible with the resources available. It is measurable progress and indicates what you plan to achieve in one budget cycle.

Using some of the same issues that helped illustrate how goals are derived from an issue statement, in the examples below I will merely add objectives that are more measurable and time-specific. As you read the issue, notice how the goals naturally cascade from the data and issue statement, and that annual objectives are merely more measurable extensions of the goals. Each objective establishes an expectation of what will be accomplished in that budget cycle.

Note: For the objectives, all are assumed to be accomplished by the end of the fiscal year. Typically, all objectives have due dates, as later examples will show.

Example #1

> Erroneous radio reads from water meters (575 out of 462,433 billings) for an average cost of $804.23 per error (over $460,000 in additional cost), continue to create billing adjustments, increase costs, reduce efficiency, lower productivity, and loss of Department credibility. Great progress was made during the past year, but the Customer Service Section anticipates ongoing issues with meters that were programmed by personnel prior to receiving proper training or with meters that have defective radio read equipment. These factors increase the number of customer contacts (it takes an average of 2 hours staff time per adjustment), increase backlog, facilitate errors, and limit the ability to provide quality financial data.

Goal 1: To reduce the number of erroneous meter reads

> Objective: To reduce, from 575 to <450, the number of erroneous radio meter reads occurring annually, by (date).

Goal 2: To reduce the annual error cost associated with erroneous reads

> Objective: To reduce, from nearly $460,000 to <$360,000, the total annual error cost associated with erroneous radio meter reads, by (date).

Example #2

> Childhood immunization rates have fallen from 83% to <60% since 2005, while the number of reported cases of school days lost due to mumps, measles, and whooping cough have increased by 312% statewide. The CDC recommends a minimum of 80% immunization rates to avoid epidemics among school-age children. Higher disease levels have increased medical costs for families, increased health risks associated with childhood diseases, jeopardized federal funding, and created a difficult teaching/learning environment due to large numbers of absent students.

Goal 1: To increase immunization rates among the K–3 school population base.

> Objective: To increase, from <60% to >66%, the immunization rates among the K–3 school population base, by (date).

Goal 2: To reduce the number of school days lost due to preventable childhood diseases.

> Objective: To reduce, from 3,416 to <2,000 the number of school days lost due to preventable childhood diseases, by (date).

Example #3

> A major type of reported criminal offense is personal property
> crime and includes theft, vandalism and burglary. In 2010,
> there were a combined total of 1,429 personal property type
> crimes, almost 70% of the total reported offenses. This is a
> 57% increase in property crime in the past three years. This
> growth has increased case backlog by over 30%, reduced
> resources available for patrol and investigation, increased
> overtime costs, reduced time spent on each case, impacted
> case solvability and property recovery, and has created image
> problems for the City—a potential negative for economic
> development.

Goal 1: To reduce the number of personal property crimes occurring in
the City.

> Objective: To reduce, from 70% to <50% of total reported
> offenses, the number of personal property crimes occurring in
> the City, by (date).

Goal 2: To reduce the case backlog of personal property crimes

> Objective: To reduce, from 63 cases to <40 cases per officer,
> the case backlog of personal property crimes, by (date).

Goal 3: To reduce the total operating costs associated with personal
property crimes

> Objective: To reduce, from $1,557,500 to <$1,475,000 the
> total operating costs associated with personal property
> crimes, by (date).

If you collect and analyze data, you will have the basis for measuring
progress. Many will ask (or complain) about the danger of stating a
numeric performance measure that might not be achieved or achievable.
This could be due to insufficient budget allocation or staff resources to
accomplish the annual objective. I have been there and empathize.

However, the assumption is that if additional funds or FTEs are required, they will be listed in your strategies and actions. Acquiring money and staff resources is *not* a goal or objective—it is a strategy or action. The underlying assumption is that if you do not receive adequate funding or human resources, achieving your stated objective will be doubtful. As a professional, however, you must still establish goals and objectives and do your best. When you complete your Annual Variance Report (discussed in Part V) you will explain what was and was not achieved and state the reason for any variance.

Outputs and Outcomes

Accountability is essential in government. Never before have there been so many questions about the value vs. cost of public programs and these questions will continue to grow more complex. For strategic planners, which in my view includes all elected officials, administrators, and managers, the challenge lies in expressing clear goals and measured objectives. A key word in public management is *performance*. Good objectives contain performance measures and clearly indicate planned progress toward goals. Keep the following definitions in mind:

> **Performance Standards** = Targeted performance expressed as measured criteria against which actual achievement is compared. Performance measures are found in properly written objectives.

There are many ways of expressing objectives. However, objectives are either *output* measures or *outcome* measures. The objective is not to undertake the action; it is to achieve a measured result—a desired, calculated output or outcome as defined below.

> **Output Measures** = Program outputs that can be counted as a measure of what was accomplished; The number of services provided, programs delivered, people served, miles paved, licenses renewed, housing permits distributed, people trained, cases worked, assessments completed, meters read, systems renovated, sidewalks repaired, people screened, immunizations provided, etc.

Outcome Measures = Assessment of *actual impact* of actions; measured achievements that address the issue. Outcome objectives seek to reduce recidivism, juvenile crime, gang activity, transaction cost, heart attacks, obesity, traffic deaths, etc. They may seek to increase park or library usage, economic growth, graduation rates, reading scores, program participation, etc.

Understanding the difference between outputs and outcomes is critical. Both are important and are essential to good strategic planning. Most participants in my strategic planning seminars understand outputs very quickly and can generate a list of typical outputs within thirty minutes. Begin with the issue and goal then move to the objective. If you want to demonstrate progress toward a longer-term goal, an output objective is often the best means of establishing your intent and a means of measuring progress. Below are examples taken from various state and local government plans.

Output Measures – Examples

- Increased number of road miles with new divider lines and intersections with 4-way stop signs

- Increased number of community policing programs provided

- Increased number of people trained in a specific subject

- Increased number of miles patrolled by police officers or Sheriff deputies

- Increased number of parks renovated

- Increased or total number of miles of wastewater pipe inspected

- Number of new recycling pickup areas established

- Increase in miles of sidewalks repaired to ADA standards

- Number of annual housing inspections

- Total number of streams and water bodies evaluated

- Reduced number of property (and other) crimes in areas with strong patrol presence

- Number of K–3 kids immunized for DPT

- Number of people screened for hypertension

- Number of firemen EMT trained

- Increase in the number of citizens attending programs about property tax increases

- Increased signage and lower speed limits in residential areas

Outcome Measures – Examples

- Reduced number of children with mumps, measles and rubella; fewer school days lost

- Reduction in traffic accidents blamed on poor signage or unmarked 4-way intersections

- Greater community cooperation with a variety of law enforcement efforts; harmony/support

- Increase in productivity or quality due to training

- Reduced cost per transaction due to new software and training

- Reduced error rate due to various innovative actions

- Reduced number of heart attacks and strokes due to increased screening

- Increased number of people saved by firemen providing early intervention

- Reduced number of complaints from the public and greater efficiency for Assessor's staff

- Reduced number of accidents and serious incidents occurring in neighborhoods

As you contemplate desired outputs and outcomes, ask, 'What are we trying to achieve? If we complete one or more actions, what result will the community or stakeholders most likely see?

Some objectives are proactive outputs intended to generate progress toward goals and to address an issue. These are the most common objectives due to the ability of program administrators and department directors to establish outputs designed to meet a need or solve a problem. However, it is unfortunate that most fail to insert actual measurement into the objective statement, such as '*To increase, from 74 to at least 90, the number of lane-miles with upgraded signage.*' Otherwise, it becomes a general activity statement that has no measurement or intended annual output. As a senior administrator, I want to *know* what that program is going to accomplish in the coming year. I don't want a general statement telling me that "We are increasing signage in the south section of the city." Okay, but by how much and from what number to what number?

Outcomes represent the *actual impact* desired and achieved from the strategies and actions listed under the objective. If you increased the number of employees trained in the new software from 8 to 20 and now all are trained, what was the result? Did anything accrue from this costly effort? If your objective was '*To increase, from 4 to 8, the number of transactions per FTE in the same time period*' then you achieved a desired *productivity outcome*. If you reduced the number of highway deaths, obesity levels, and the number of children contracting preventable diseases, those are all important *status outcomes*.

As an elected executive, administrator or program manager, when you review the issues and associated data, what important outputs and/or outcomes can you identify? After reviewing the issue, goals should be easy because they require no data. Objectives require more thought because you must employ data to determine what outputs or outcomes are desired and possible and what measures are appropriate.

Maintenance Goals and Objectives

Mentioned several times in the preceding sections are maintenance goals and objectives. These are simply the goals and objectives that clarify what values or standards you want to maintain. They are important because they establish parameters and announce your intent to maintain them. Some are internal; others are mandated, such as EPA air and water quality standards. Others come from professional associations, such as the American Water Works Association, American Public Works Association, National Fire Academy, or the National Association of Police Planners.

Most large public agencies have internal or external standards that benchmark basic performance. Unfortunately, many smaller agencies do not have clear standards that describe what constitutes core performance. Once you have achieved a standard, the long-term goal and annual objective is to maintain it. I have never found a federal, state or local government agency, board, commission or program that has no maintenance goals and objectives.

What are the most essential standards that must be maintained and are of strategic importance to the agency, constituents or community? Take time in a planning group to identity key areas that have standards then identify the standards. Many already exist in performance budgets or in current planning documents. There are several maintenance objectives in the following general examples.

General Examples – Objectives

The following are random examples pulled from various plans. For some, I have added notations or explanations. All are properly crafted.

- To increase, from 420 to at least 475, the number of lane-miles resurfaced within the city limits; evaluated by ___. (output)

- To reduce, by at least 25%, the number of serious auto accidents occurring at county intersections; evaluated by ___. Or... To reduce, from 32 to <20, the number of serious auto accidents occurring at county intersections; evaluated by ___. (It is always best to go from a number to a number if you track data.)

- To increase, from 13 to at least 20, the number of shop employees who are certified in MIG and TIG welding; by _____. (output)

- To reduce, from an average of 3.75 hours to <2.25 hours, the time required to complete X-12 projects requiring MIG or TIG welds; by _____. (outcome)

- To reduce, by at least 10%, the time required to process DT-105 forms; by _____.

- To reduce, from 18 to <6, the number of personal injury automobile accidents occurring on Interstate 70 between Kansas City and St. Louis, by _____. (outcome)

- To increase, from 7 to at least 10, the number of staff engineers who complete their PE designation by _____. (output)

- To maintain, at 15 minutes or less, the average response time for any emergency waste treatment system trouble call, evaluated monthly.

- To maintain normal filter run times of no more than 120 hours in the West Treatment Plant; evaluated annually.

- To maintain the electrical consumption at no more than 1,036 kilowatt-hours per million gallons of water pumped from Ashcroft to Overshoe; evaluated annually.

- To maintain at 6 minutes or less, the average EMS response time to an emergency call within county limits; evaluated quarterly.

Summary

Goals and objectives are the heart and soul of strategic plans. For public agencies, they declare the intent to progress and perform. Objectives announce measured progress toward goals and goals announce the intent to address stated issues.

For every public manager, the challenge is to understand the value and articulation of measurement. Words like 'improve' denote the intent to progress but do not convey the intent to increase or reduce a value. As an administrator or elected official, you must announce the issue, express current status, and present the intent to change the situation. 'Here is where we are, here is where we plan to be, and this is how we'll measure progress.' If there are standards that must be met or have been achieved and established as annual benchmarks, the long-term goal and annual objective is '*To maintain*' that standard.

Neither goals nor objectives explain *how* they will increase, reduce or maintain an expressed value. They don't explain *how* the issue will be addressed. That is the purpose of strategies and actions, which follow each objective. If you take time to define issues and challenges by utilizing accurate data, goals will quickly become apparent. Annual objectives will also be apparent but will take more time to craft due to the need for sensible metrics. How much can you achieve in the coming year? How much progress can be made toward the goal? What are you willing to risk when you identify measured progress that translates to performance?

The rule of thumb is to establish objectives based on what you believe you can achieve *and* based on the assumption that your listed strategies and actions will be funded. This is a huge question because many administrators set low goals and attainable objectives because they fear repercussions or are convinced they will not get proper funding to address the issue. Don't take this approach.

Openly state critical issues, establish sensible goals, and establish objectives with good metrics. List appropriate strategies and actions that you and your team believe are necessary to address the stated issue(s). If funding is required, make it one of your strategies. If it remains unfunded, that is out of your hands. Elected officials are faced with the confluence of enormously complex problems and finite revenues, so must triage every funding request. You may not receive funding but you have done your professional duty by clearly describing major issues, establishing goals and objectives and suggesting appropriate strategies and actions. In doing so, you are also on record and have clearly expressed the probability and magnitude of impact to citizens.

How the request is evaluated among other priorities is out of the department or program administrator's hands once budget requests are formalized. Strong, data-driven issue statements tend to get attention and funding. This is a difficult aspect of public management. Always err on the side of quality planning and professional recommendations. You have done your part and have signaled your readiness to perform.

Chapter 15

Strategies and Actions

Based on the earlier review of planning psychology and the human tendency to think in action terms, this plan element is perhaps the most commonly understood. In fact, most groups inadvertently begin with strategies and actions, then work backward to identify goals and objectives. As professionals who work in the arena every day, they *know* what needs to be done to achieve success. Typically, most have a lot of experience developing strategies and actions as part of normal operations. While many do not initially link to issues, goals and annual objectives, managers can quickly agree on the appropriate actions required to achieve results.

The most challenging aspect of this section is the *differentiation* between *strategies* and *actions*. The former is a general approach; the latter is a specific activity. Some plans combine strategies and actions into one set of actions/strategies. This works well and can save time quibbling over whether the chosen activity is a strategy or an underlying action. The classic strategic plan 'fishbone' diagram identifies both.

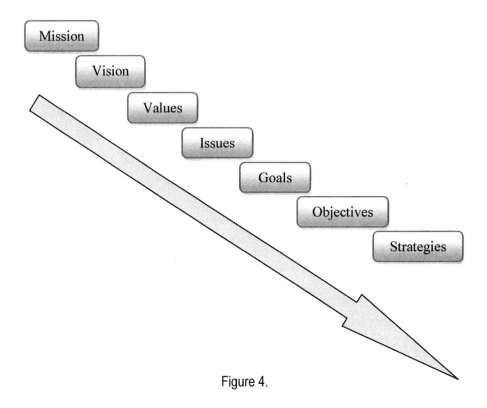

Figure 4.

Classic planning is done sequentially; each element either provides a basis for general understanding or provides underpinning for the next element. A mission introduces why the agency or program exists and briefly explains what it does; in so doing it provides insight for the reader about *purpose*. An objective expresses what the intended progress will be toward a longer-term goal. An action provides a specific step toward accomplishing a more general strategy.

Some managers resist detailing *both* strategies and actions due to the additional work involved. But there is little doubt that the best, most comprehensive plans have both elements. For the most part, both strategies and actions represent keys to achievement. They express how the agency plans to accomplish goals and objectives and address strategic issues. *Strategies and actions cost money.* You can have the most aggressive goals and objectives possible and they will not cost a penny until you detail the accompanying strategies and actions. They are the interface point between the plan and the budget. This is an essential point that deserves an example.

Years ago, while serving as a state public health education director I encountered very low immunization rates. To address this issue, I established the goal, '*To increase immunization rates for preventable childhood diseases in the K–3 school-age population.*' Establishing this goal cost the state nothing. My first year objective was, '*To increase, from 62% to >70%, the immunization rates for preventable childhood diseases in the K–3 school-age population.*' (Successive annual objectives ended well above 80%.) This aggressive objective also cost nothing. While I don't have the space to convey the total Immunization Action Plan, one strategy will perhaps serve as an illustration.

One important *strategy* was to 'Develop a comprehensive statewide media and public awareness campaign targeting parents of school-age children.' As noted earlier, a strategy is broad and general; it expresses at least one general approach and, in this case, involved a statewide media and public awareness campaign. If my plan had only contained this general strategy, there would have been nothing to support the overall campaign budget request or to sell my ideas to the state health officer, Joint Finance and Appropriations Committee, and Governor. To accomplish the plan, I had to explain two things: the most important intended actions that took time and money, and the projected outcome. Some of the most important *actions* that accompanied the general strategy were:

- Hold multiple meetings with the print and electronic media throughout the state.

- Draft and have the governor sign a proclamation supporting 'Immunization Action Month.'

- Meet with the state medical association and local physicians throughout the state.

- Contract with artists and designers to develop posters, brochures and flyers for use during the campaign.

- Purchase a variety of germane materials from private suppliers and order materials from the CDC in Atlanta.

- Travel statewide to meet with school districts and local PTA/ PTO organizations to enlist their help with the campaign.

- Organize a series of 'Immunization Action' Basketball tournaments to generate awareness.

- Develop and execute a mass mailing campaign to coincide with the media campaign.

There were many more individual actions and sub-actions that cost time and money and all were part of the general strategy (the Immunization Action Basketball Tournament alone was a huge project that required many sub-actions). *All actions had due dates and were sequential.* Taken together, they comprised the overall Immunization *Action Plan* that was a specific budget item and represented a major strategic commitment for my bureau, the department and the Office of the Governor. I am proud to say that the state's immunization rates were raised to significantly high levels within three years, and met all established goals.

Recommendation: Consider selecting only essential strategies and perhaps several important actions under each, making it clear to managers that individual programs must have detailed action plans contained in their Operations Plans. This allows an interface between strategic and operations plans and keeps a lot of operational activities out of the strategic plan. Place a note in the strategic plan announcing that 'Additional detail is found in the (department/bureau) operating plan.'

Keep in mind that issues are *why* you are taking action; goals and objectives express *what* you intend to accomplish; and strategies and actions explain *how* you plan to accomplish goals and objectives. As you begin identifying strategies and actions, keep the following in mind:

- Strategies and actions provide a path to achievement.

- Strategies and actions follow each objective; they are the means to achieve objectives.

- They are short, concise, descriptive, actions phrases.

- There is no limit to the number of strategies or actions you can place under an objective but you may want to share the most important and maintain more detailed action plans in a separate document.

- Strategies and actions describe *how and when* you plan to achieve objectives; actions should have start dates and/or due dates.

- Actions may state who's responsible (Champions or Owners); this is *strongly recommended* for accountability.

- Strategies and actions tie to your budget; they cost money and will relate directly to decision units and/or program performance expectations.

- Performance budgets tie directly to annual objectives, strategies and actions.

- Strategies and actions when compiled will comprise your action plan, i.e. how you will achieve program objectives.

- Ideally, actions should be sequential, prioritized, and clarify *who* will do *what, where,* and by *when;* most managers are reluctant to name accountable parties, but it is advisable unless an entire work unit is responsible.

- Knowing you will have an Annual Variance or Progress Report, establish an evaluation process that discusses review frequency, how achievement is verified, and how you will demonstrate proper execution of actions.

When considering strategic issues — not general core operations — funding requests must always relate to strategies and actions, which in turn relate to both goals and objectives. This is what ties the strategic plan to the budget. Goals and objectives cost nothing; it is strategies and actions that demonstrate how you will address issues. They cost time and money and are therefore a key element of a budget request.

Selecting Strategies and Actions

When I work with public agencies to review their plans, managers very quickly identify the variety of strategies and actions that are misstated as 'goals' and 'objectives.' This is important because those organizations have therefore already identified many key strategies and actions they plan to implement; they just have not determined the ultimate goals and annual objectives. This is common and acceptable. It provides the ability to 'back into' goals and objectives by asking the most important question in planning:

The Most Important Word in Planning

Many years ago in a rugged northwestern state I was taking a group of highway maintenance workers through a planning exercise. The leader was around 6' 7" tall and weighed at least 290. These were tough guys and I had to lead them through a strategic thinking process to develop a decent plan. After listening to my spiel for an hour, they informed me that they already had an objective and proudly showed it to me. It was, 'To purchase 500 gallons of yellow paint and move it to Tretonville by July 1st.' They had numbers, a date and it began with 'To.' I realized I had to help them understand that this was indeed an action, because it did not increase, reduce or maintain anything, plus the action cost money and had the action, 'To purchase.' It was clearly not the objective.

So, I used the most important word in public planning: *Why?* If you had the paint, what problem would it solve? What would you do with it and what would it achieve? In other words, *why* are you purchasing the paint? They got a bit grumpy, but after some debate seemed to grasp what I was trying to convey. They retired to another room to deliberate and emerged minutes later proudly proclaiming that they had identified the true objective and were sorry for the confusion. The revised objective read:

'To paint yellow lines on fifteen miles of highway from Tretonville to Wineville before July 1st.' They related how they *now* understood that purchasing the paint was an action and the real objective was *to paint* the yellow lines.

I was challenged because I again had to ask the critical question, '*Why?*' It was clear that *to paint* was another action and I still had to help them discover the real objective. It was important for them to understand that painting lines on the highway was merely an activity to help achieve *something*. So, I forged ahead and asked the question, '*Why* would you paint lines on that stretch of highway?' Boy, did they get mad!

For a few minutes I thought they were going to throw me out in the snow and they did, in fact, become quite verbal. In this heated moment the foreman loudly exclaimed, "Listen, there have been a lot of accidents on that stretch of road, and..." I immediately interrupted, saying, "Oh...accidents? How many? Is that why you are painting yellow lines?" He glared at me for a moment, but I could see he was beginning to connect the dots. As an experienced professional, his focus was on operating actions and not on underlying issues, goals or objectives. He gathered his men and quietly moved to the next room.

A few minutes later, they returned and he told me that they now understood the objective was, and read it to me: "To reduce, from 22 to less than 12, the number of serious injury automobile accidents occurring on Highway 67 between Tretonville and Wineville, by (date)." Yes! A decent objective; We then discussed that buying paint, painting yellow lines, doing shoulder and crown work, installing new guard rails, pruning foliage on blind corners, etc. were all actions that contributed to the objective and goal. Actions were the operations part of their work that enabled them to achieve the objective. The issue was the number of serious auto accidents on that stretch of highway and the long-term goal was 'To reduce the number of serious injury automobile accidents occurring on state highways.'

I have changed city and highway names, but this example represents a common experience. After conducting planning programs for virtually every facet of state and local government, I have found that managers tend to aggregate strategies and actions as their principal planning exercise. By asking 'Why?,' it is reasonably simple to identify issues, goals and objectives. If an organization has lists of actions that have erroneously been termed goals and objectives, the first order of business is to ask why they are doing those things. After training, most administrators, managers, and supervisors will quickly return to their plans and within a short time use their strategies and actions to properly identify and articulate goals and objectives.

An Elected Prerogative

For readers who are elected officials, the question, 'Why?' is essential. While it can be misused, it can also be the most important tool in your tool kit when trying to determine the value of a program or recommended effort. When speaking to city managers, mayors, city councils, commissions, aldermen, legislators, etc. I encourage them to recognize actions that cost money and ask why they are being done. What is the underlying issue? Why is it critical from an operational or strategic standpoint? Why are you employing this particular strategy or series of actions as opposed to others? And, if there are no associated goals or objectives that reflect the intent to increase or reduce a serious condition or maintain an important standard, why are you spending money on these actions?

Administrators may recoil at this recommendation. However, there is enormous value in properly constructed public plans that convey strategic issues, express goals and measurable objectives, and suggest appropriate strategies and actions that address the issue and show progress. Strong issue statements that express magnitude of impact and consequence provide rationale for budgeted strategies and actions. Elected officials are generally not subject matter experts but must rely on internal (and sometimes external) professionals. By asking *Why,* they signal their interest and willingness to understand issues. They also convey their resolve to ensure that any funded strategy or action be directly connected to a meaningful issue and that goals and measurable objectives have been established to measure progress. This is what good public management is all about.

Whenever an action word other than increase, reduce or maintain is seen in a strategic plan as part of a goal or objective, ask WHY? Why are you painting, installing, convening, purchasing, hiring, developing, improving, training etc.? The answer will be the actual goal or objective, which will increase, reduce, or maintain some numeric value.

If additional funds or FTEs are required, they will be listed in your strategies and actions. Acquiring money and staff resources is not a goal or objective—it is a strategy or action. The understanding is that if you do not receive adequate funding or human resources, achieving your stated objective will be doubtful. As a professional, however, you will still establish goals and objectives and do your best to accomplish them.

Chapter 16

Strategic Initiatives

There is always risk associated with adding plan sections that are anomalies. However, strategic initiatives are an exception. This language is common in both business and public planning and helps identify the major initiatives considered essential for organization or community progress.

Strategic initiatives are typically major internal or external actions that require significant amounts of time, money and manpower. They are important to an agency, its constituents or the entire community, and may result from years of planning to address a long-standing issue. Every state and local government regularly undertakes major strategic initiatives but rarely are they properly identified. Generally, strategic initiatives:

- Address major issues that have been evaluated over time.

- Are significant undertakings that require a great deal of time, money and effort.

- Require one to several years to complete.

- Deal with major changes, additions, rebuilding, renovation, transitions, new systems, etc.

- May impact several departments, programs, constituent groups, an entire community or state.

- Have major budget impact and must be planned in advance.

- Require elected decision-maker approval through executive, legislative or budget processes.

- Are undertaken to provide significant improvements.

Strategic initiatives can be prompted by the need to make important internal improvements or are driven by external issues and challenges. There are often questions regarding what constitutes a strategic initiative as opposed to a normal action. Fundamentally, it is *magnitude*. If you have had efficiency issues attributed to your bureau's software program and have determined that the best fix is new software, the decision-making, cost, implementation and efficiency improvement is generally localized. If, however, a two-year analysis has determined that a county's or city's overall productivity and efficiency is substandard and that a variety of major improvements could be realized through an entirely new information technology system, the changeover becomes a *major initiative* that has broad, long-term and strategic consequences.

Don't be confused by the reality that the initiative is operational in nature and that it is merely a really big action. It remains an operational action but it addresses a major internal issue and will make a significant *contribution* to the organization. If upgrading the city's entire information system produces potent new efficiencies, increases productivity, reduces complaints, reduces backlog, shortens transaction time, and lowers cost to taxpayers, it is a major strategic initiative that is warranted and will probably enjoy broad support. Replacing a few vehicles is not a strategic initiative; upgrading an entire fleet might have strategic consequences. *It is a question of magnitude and contribution.*

Those who have endured major system evolutions can attest to the magnitude of such events and that significant prior planning was done before the final decision was made. After a 'Go' decision, planning, execution, implementation, training and full burn-in might take two or more years. Costs may exceed several million dollars and many human resources will ultimately be engaged. In other words, it is *major*. It is strategic because of its broad application to all agencies and to their ability to provide efficient, effective services to citizens.

External issues and challenges are often so large or pervasive that major initiatives are required to address them. For instance, Cowlitz County, Washington has done a remarkable job analyzing its long-term solid waste requirements compared to current landfill capacity. After years of study and planning, the County embarked on a five-year transition to another landfill that will be privately managed. The County will over time transition out of much of the solid waste management business but will retain oversight. A portion of its strategic plan states:

> Due to continued growth and accelerated use, the Cowlitz County Landfill is expected to be full by late 2012, leaving few cost effective options for waste disposal. Trips per day have increased by 45% since 1995 and total tonnage has grown from 6,900 tons per month to over 9,185 tons per month. Similarly, total operating cost increased from $1.15 million in 1995 to over $2.2 million in 2007. In November 2006, Cowlitz County entered into a long-term contract with Waste Control Recycling to provide for solid waste transport and disposal out of the County once the landfill reaches capacity in late 2012. The agreement calls for phased transition of services from public to private operations between 2008 and 2012. This private-public partnership is now a *Major Strategic Initiative* (italics added) for the Department of Public Works.

> As the landfill reaches capacity, it will undergo closure construction and transition into post-closure care and monitoring. With other major County priorities, it is clear that insufficient planning, on-site logistics, design, regulatory review and contract preparation would pose a serious impediment to a cost-effective transition that will protect the public and provide promised service levels far into the future. The challenge will be to implement the overall plan carefully and fully to minimize monetary impact to reserve accounts

established for these purposes and to provide for an environmentally sound closure that preserves the public trust.

Transitioning to a privately managed landfill system is a classic *external* strategic initiative. It took significant analysis, planning, negotiation, budgeting and administration. It is long-term, requires careful fiscal management, and many professional staff hours. Most importantly, it will address several major issues and provide broad, long-term benefits to county residents.

Identifying Strategic Initiatives

During issue identification, you will discover a variety of significant problems and challenges that may require major initiatives. Most administrators already know the most important actions that need to be undertaken to improve the organization or community. They will already know most, if not all of the major initiatives that would address external issues. Most have been discussed for several budget cycles and many have been recommended in prior years.

Keep in mind that strategic initiatives are *comprehensive* projects that address important internal or external issues. In a properly conducted planning exercise, internal and external issues will be identified and prioritized according to magnitude, relevance, and impact; cost does *not* enter into discussions about priority. That is a budgeting decision. The real questions pertain to how significant the issue/problem is, what is the downside to not addressing it, and what benefits will accrue from addressing it. To identify strategic initiatives, I suggest the following:

- Use the normal issue identification process to identify issues and problems.

- As part of that process, identify both internal and external issues.

- For each, assess the magnitude of the problem using gathered data.

- Determine if there are already recommended initiatives to address major internal and external issues; if there are, annotate them using preexisting documentation, analysis and proposed actions.

- Determine all major initiatives that would stand alone as important improvement projects, writing the essence of the proposed solution; at this point don't try to write a complete statement. Just identify the essence.

- Working within channels, agree on major *internal* strategic initiatives that administrators and managers want in the plan and for which they are willing to either allocate existing funds or seek new resources.

- Working again within channels, agree on major *external* strategic initiatives that administrators want in the plan and for which they are willing to allocate existing funds or will seek new funding.

On an annual basis, there are not many strategic initiatives. The danger is overstating general operational actions, implying they are highly significant when they are merely important but can still be addressed internally through existing program efforts. When included in a strategic plan, the reader should be able to quickly grasp the significance of the issue and understand the value of the proposed initiative. Each major strategic initiative must tie to an issue that is listed in the plan, either at the agency or executive level. Building a new county courthouse is not an agency level initiative. It resides with the commission and voters. But, there may be genuinely supportable rationale for a new courthouse and various associated issues, each with very strong data.

Similarly, there are pervasive internal issues that can only be addressed by major actions, such as building a new police station, jail or library, or implementing an entirely new county-wide EMS communication system. All are time consuming, important, and costly initiatives that have strategic consequences for either an agency or the community, or both.

Writing Strategic Initiatives

This unique plan element is written as a 'mini' project overview. It describes project scope, addresses resource requirements, provides a timeline and outlines expected benefits. It is brief, concise and clear. Below are examples of internal and external improvement *initiatives*.

Example #1

> Initiate a system-wide upgrade of the state Revenue and Taxation Department's recordkeeping system to include hardware upgrades and replacing current system software; analyze total system needs by 9/2011; create a total refinement plan by 12/2011; prepare bids and announce by 5/2012; select and contract with vendors by 8/2012; complete vendor analysis by 10/2012; begin transition planning by 1/2013; fully implement hardware and software transition by 10/2013; complete training and burn-in by 4/2014; have full system in place and operating effectively by 7/2014. Total cost: $3.25 million over four years. Anticipate 12% productivity gain, 18% efficiency gain, and >$500,000 reduction in annual operating costs.

Example #2

> Plan, develop and implement an 800 MHz radio system throughout the county for use by all public safety agencies; develop and let bids, select vendors, complete planning, build four towers, equip, test and have on-line by 7/2014. Estimated cost: $2.37 million over three years and increase of $78,000 in annual operations, with no additional FTEs. The system will expand coverage, reduce dead zones, increase collaboration, and reduce response times. Corollary benefits include better insurance rates, less property damage during fires (response time value), and more medical emergencies resulting in saved lives.

A comprehensive project plan requires dozens of pages with detailed support data and financials. It does not belong in the strategic plan. A strategic initiative is a short, encapsulated overview that offers a thumbnail sketch of what is intended, when, at what cost and the benefit expected. The Cowlitz County solid waste strategic initiative is a good external example. It is a large, complex issue that has many aspects—environmental, fiscal, operational, logistical, public image, utilization, etc. There is a clear issue with comprehensive support data providing rationale, a long-range plan with milestones, and clear benefits to the County. Even though the entire transition plan contains many pages, the strategic initiative is short, clear and powerful.

Again, what major projects do you want to showcase in your plan? What will provide the most benefit for overall government, a department, or the entire community? If you are building a new courthouse, upgrading the waste treatment plant, building a new water plant, upgrading your internal data collection system, replacing the classification and compensation system, etc., you may want to provide a powerful description in a strategic initiatives section and have strongly worded, persuasive, issue statements that provide rationale for the initiatives.

Location in the Plan

In smaller agency, division and bureau plans, strategic initiatives are typically placed after the section containing all goals, objectives, strategies and actions. They require a separate section to emphasize their importance and to focus the reader's attention.

For larger organizations that provide a strategic plan summary of Agency Goals, Major Challenge Areas (significant issues) and Major Contributions, it is best to also include a section showcasing Major Strategic Initiatives. This is generally done at the department level or for the entire state, city or county government. For very large divisions within even larger departments, this is also a good method.

Remember that you are showcasing major initiatives that will involve significant internal or external effort. The initiatives have strategic value and, if accomplished, will make measurable contributions to the community or specific stakeholders.

Some plan components are traditional and essential. In modern state and local government, strategic initiatives have become critical elements of every plan. They allow the government and every agency to 'showcase' the most important internal and external projects with linkage to carefully vetted problem statements. Keep in mind that *initiatives* are projects; they are large-scale activities that cost a lot of money and are undertaken to provide measurable benefit. They are issue-driven and, if accomplished, will improve the value of government services and their impact on the community.

Chapter 17

Compiling a Total Document

This short chapter addresses questions raised about what constitutes appropriate content in a complete department plan. A common question is, 'What is the plan supposed to look like when it's done?' Due to formatting and presentation preferences the final 'look' is impossible to dictate. Content, on the other hand, is much easier.

The actual strategic plan will have specific components that include mission, vision, operating philosophy/values, issues and challenges, long-term goals, annual objectives, strategies and actions. These have been described in great detail in Parts III and IV. However, to present a truly potent and comprehensive document, there are other elements that I suggest for every department in state and local government.

Many readers are familiar with planning documents and have prepared or are familiar with the sections suggested below. However, always keep in mind that both *what* you place in the plan and *how* you present the information become pivotal elements of your story. Remember that a department plan is a compilation of all section, bureau and division plans. Summary 'up front' sections provide an overview of various issues/challenges, overarching goals, contributions, strategic initiatives, etc. The detail is found in individual division plans. Elements of a strong department plan should include:

Letter from the Director – An upbeat professional message that introduces the document, explains its purpose, and expresses appreciation for employee, and perhaps community, involvement.

Preface and Acknowledgements – A short review of what the document contains and laudatory comments about those who committed time and energy to the process. I always include a list of the strategic planning team, editing team and any community organizations or individuals groups that assisted with plan development.

Organization Chart – A general chart depicting major operational elements of the department; stay general but include all elements that have a stand-alone plan in the compiled document.

Overview of the Strategic Planning Process – Explains the strategic planning process and what the department went through to produce the plan. This will include sequential steps, timeline, actions taken, and generally how the plan was compiled. This is a good place to review the department's planning philosophy and commitment to strategic thinking and planning for the future.

Department Mission, Vision and Values – Typically placed on one page with an attractive layout, the overall department Mission, Vision, and Values are presented as representative, all-encompassing statements. In their plans, each division and bureau/section may still present their individual statements, but all should connect with the department's or government's central themes.

Department Focus Areas (or Major Goals) – A review of the 8 to 12 goals or *focus areas* are chosen by the department director or senior management team. Some organizations choose to list as goals; others list as 'focus areas.' However, this is an important listing that identifies those topical areas that are high priority to the department...and to elected officials.

Department Achievements and Contributions – Describing historic achievement and contributions is an important part of a department's story. This section provides a brief review of various accomplishments achieved over the past several years. It is helpful to present achievements of each division to showcase the origin and nature of their diverse contributions. Do not embellish; instead err on the side of a 'clinical' review, using good data coupled with a brief description.

Major Challenge Areas and Trends – This is an important summary element of the overall plan because it compiles the major issues and challenges that the department is facing. These are generally external issues and challenges but can include significant internal challenges that inhibit the department's ability to achieve its mission. Departments are wise to share information on major challenges along with trend information that depicts the probability and impact associated with predictable events or troubling situations.

Major Strategic Initiatives – Every department has major strategic initiatives either underway or that it plans to undertake. It is important to showcase these each year. Many of these are already funded and enjoy support from elected officials. There are always questions pertaining to where a department is allocating resources. This summarizes all key initiatives and provides a brief review.

Organization Improvement Initiatives – This section addresses critical internal issues identified in previous years and shares information about what the department is doing to remedy them. While there may be a separate *Improvement Plan*, the strategic plan can summarize any initiative dedicated to continuous process, program, or organizational improvement.

Introduction to Division Plans – Always provide a review of division plans and explain what each division strategic plan contains. Department strategic plans are merely composites of division (and perhaps bureau) plans; an overview of division plan content and format explains how and why those plans were formulated. If you use a special format, this section is the perfect place to explain it and how to interpret it.

Division Strategic Plans – This is the largest section of the overall document because it contains all division strategic plans. For large departments, there could be 15 or more separate division plans, each a stand-alone document. Provide a divider page that separates the previously listed pages and 'up front' summaries from the actual division plans.

The 'up-front' sections work equally well for a comprehensive city or county plan where individual department plans comprise most of the content. State plans are somewhat different, but typically follow a similar format.

Presenting a strategic plan is more art than science. If all division and bureau plans are properly developed, it is a simple matter to prepare summaries at the department level. The questions are: *What are the major challenges we are facing that need to be reviewed early in the overall plan? What are the most significant contributions and achievements the department would like to share with the public? What is the department's focus over the next year or two? And, what are the department's mission, vision, and values?*

Whether you term these up-front, summary, or roll-up sections, they add critical elements to your plan. To present an independent overview, some plans provide separately bound documents containing information on trends and major challenges. Others prefer to combine all division plans (or department plans, if the overall document is for a state, city or county) with the up-front summary sections. However you choose to present plan content, I encourage you to include the content listed above. It will ensure that you are able to convey a complete and powerful story about the organization.

Final Thoughts – Part IV

As promised, Part IV combines a mix of classic strategic plan language, approaches and formatting with new perspectives and approaches to public sector planning. Throughout the section, the greatest emphasis has been on understanding. While there have been various approaches to strategic thinking and plan development for state and local government, their origin has not been deeply rooted in public issues and challenges. Those who have not labored in city, county or state government have little understanding of the pressures, obstacles, and limits placed on public employees and elected officials. They also have not had the opportunity to dissect language associated with missions, issue statements, goals and objectives and apply perspectives that match the inherent realities of everyday agency or municipal life. *Connecting that reality to the growing expectations of a restless public is the ultimate challenge.*

Aside from language and perspective, the most important message contained in Part IV is the need to understand how data associated with public and organizational issues drive the formation and value of goals and objectives. Of all the topics covered, perhaps none is more important than the need to embrace the true nature of goals and objectives. As you move to Part V, which shares a variety of implementation strategies, I encourage you to think about the simple formula introduced in Chapter 11. Very simply, as you examine the data in various topical areas, ask, 'Is this value too high? Is it too low?' Or, 'Does it meet an acceptable standard?' If you have good data (even marginal data provides a starting point), it is a simple process to engage subject matter experts to decide if the numbers have exceeded limits either over or below standards and to then establish goals that will provide a message with clear intent *to reduce* or *to increase*. And, as noted above, if experts agree that the values are acceptable, the goal is *to maintain* that standard.

Overall, it seems a minor thing. But through the years, this formula and approach has proven to be the simplest and most powerful planning tool introduced to public agencies. I hope you will give it a try. If you do, you will experience an approach that adds energy, speed and simplicity to your planning process.

Part Five

Implementing and Managing the Strategic Planning Process

Many who labored through the previous section with some attention to detail will have noticed two things. First, that they already know many of the terms, formats and approaches associated with strategic planning and second, that several nuances were introduced that will improve their planning process and product.

Redundantly perhaps, I again encourage you to embrace the concept that all *public sector* strategic plans must be *issue-driven*. A strategic plan is not an operations plan. It is a special element of executive planning that addresses the most important challenges the agency and community are facing and describes remediation strategies. It addresses probable impact and the magnitude of various issues. It does not address day-to-day operations.

The second major characteristic discussed in Parts III and IV is the very unique yet simple approach to assessing 'measurement intent.' That is, a practical perspective that encourages administrators and managers to review data, then decide if the described value is too high, too low or meets expectations. By following a linear path that gathers data, provides analysis, and assesses whether the value must be increased, reduced or maintained, public administrators will establish a platform for evaluating progress toward goals and for measuring performance. Otherwise, there is a tendency to drift toward and remain fixed on a world of composite 'To Do' lists that are *improperly* termed 'Strategic Plans.'

What vs. *how* becomes the challenge. By that, I simply mean that describing a planning system and approach is nice but doesn't contribute to implementation and management. Developing an innovative plan format and process is only the *first* step. Implementation is the most difficult part of the journey.

Over the years, experiments and trials have helped identify several practical elements of the strategic planning process. Part V contains various ancillary components of strategic plan development and implementation that will reduce heartburn and expedite integration into existing cultures. I have shared suggestions that will help organize, manage, and evaluate strategic planning in a public agency or entire government. To maintain at least some semblance of brevity, there are general suggestions that can be extrapolated to a wide variety of large or small state, city or county applications.

In today's challenging world, there is an opportunity to make strategic thinking and planning a greater positive force in the world of public administration. However, while part of the public management lexicon, it is still greatly misunderstood. A common question from elected officials and administrators regarding strategic thinking and planning pertains to how it can be institutionalized. That is, how it can become a valued part of government culture. The final chapters address that challenge and offer suggestions that will facilitate your efforts to introduce a reasonable planning process or refine an existing approach. At that point, you will have the tools to develop and integrate a process that will strengthen your ability to analyze, forecast, and plan for the many challenges that will stress state and local government in the years ahead.

By following a linear path that gathers data, provides analysis, and assesses whether the value must be increased, reduced or maintained, public administrators will establish a platform for evaluating progress toward goals and for measuring performance.

Chapter 18

Organizing the Planning Process

Planning is everyone's business. It is not the sole province of elected officials or senior administrators. The same is true for strategic thinking.

A potent workforce is one where employees continually think about how to make operations more efficient and create more value for the community. Done properly, strategic thinking and planning is an innovative, inclusive process that contributes more to an organization as more people are involved. Experience has shown that employees begin to engage when they are involved with issue and challenge identification. People like to share their input when dealing with their work and their issues. Having worked with small rural county departments with a dozen employees as well as large state departments with over 10,000 employees, I can say that engaging everyone is challenging but certainly worth the effort.

If each work unit with a specific mission is asked to develop a plan, it is much easier to get all employees engaged. It is amazing what participation can do for morale, productivity, and accountability. Keep in mind that teams are energized when they are able to identify and solve important issues; nothing builds a team more effectively than working together on issues important to the agency or the community.

Sequential Steps

Success typically depends on the ability of managers to launch the planning process in a manner that helps all employees understand what is occurring, what is going to happen, and why it is important. Far too many public (and private) organizations launch into annual planning without a timeline, zero training, and with no formal process. Others adopt a generally sensible format but do not take enough time to learn and teach the nuances.

Early in my career, while working in local and state government, I made the same mistake. I made too many assumptions and did not fully understand the need to engage and train employees early in the process. Over time, it became clear that there are specific steps that are essential milestones for every planning exercise. The following are the most important, in my experience:

Initial Mandate – It is crucial that senior elected or appointed officials establish strategic planning as an important annual or biannual event. It must have an official mandate and be considered an essential part of public administration. If embraced by a governor, mayor, city council, county commission, school board, utility district board, etc., managers and employees tend to take it more seriously. This is about *expectations*. Establish the expectation that planning is an important facet of management and will be done properly. In my view, in today's difficult times, planning is *exceptionally* important and will become even more so in the decade to come.

Announcement – If there has historically been no formal strategic planning, it is important that the intent to do so is shared. There must be a *formal* announcement that the planning process is being initiated over a specific period of time and that it will be an inclusive process involving all agencies. Invite participation throughout the organization, review the process sequence, establish a timeline, and make it clear that it is *not* optional and *will* be implemented. If outside organizations are also being engaged, they must be identified early as a formal part of the process.

Outside Facilitator – If using an outside facilitator, introduce the person early in the process. Announce and clarify the role he or she is to play, emphasizing that planning is the responsibility of each department and its various sub-divisions and that the final plan will not be written by an outside party. I believe in providing high quality training and sharing many examples, then facilitating the process rather than attempting to write plans that are best left to on-site subject matter experts. A proven strategic planning facilitator can save time and frustration—if knowledgeable, experienced in government, and if he or she has an integrated approach.

Decide Which Elements Will Have a Plan – The basic rule is to have every unit that has an independent mission develop its own plan. However, the senior administrative team must decide how deeply into the organization planning should penetrate and to what extent individual plans will be developed. Done properly, every work unit with its own mission will have a plan and the overall state, city or county plan will be compiled from completed department plans. Some executives prefer to keep planning at the department or division level, which is simpler, but reduces accountability further down in the organization. If just beginning broad-based strategic planning, it is often best to plan at the division level and above, then compile into an overall summary for the government. However you decide to proceed, this decision must be made early.

Establish a Strategic Planning Team – Select a team of individuals who will champion and help orchestrate the process in every part of the organization. Team members are selected at the beginning of the planning process and receive additional training that allows them to become in-house experts in strategic planning. It is recommended that this group be permanent within the organization structure and have a rotating membership.

Initial Training – Experience has shown that early and sustained success depends on everyone understanding the language, format, and process of strategic planning. It is critical that employees understand the differences between strategic and operations planning and how annual improvement plans are derived from both plan types. Organizations achieving the greatest success have all employees (or as many as possible) attend an initial full-day training session that details the process, plan structure, sequence, priorities, and how the plan is crafted. Secondary training will occur at the department/division level once planning begins in each part of the organization.

Provide Plan Examples – Virtually all employees like to know what the end result should look like. It is therefore very important to show examples of a good plan. Years ago, I made the mistake of launching into the process without showing completed plans that have very strong formats and great content. Remember that *content* is ultimately more critical than *format,* but it is essential that employees see and understand *one* format that is established for that government entity. Seeing how other states, cities or counties have crafted good plans always helps—as long as those samples are truly good samples and the process is accompanied by proper training and facilitation.

Begin at the Program Level – After a comprehensive training session (or sessions) for as many people as possible, begin briefing and secondary training at the work unit level (division, section, bureau, etc.). In large organizations, initial training should be conducted for all administrative and supervisory personnel in the state agency, city or county. Those individuals can then hold secondary briefings for their work units. The key is to make it an important undertaking and involve as many people as possible. I believe in teaching the process and language. The more people who understand strategic thought and can prepare sensible plans the better prepared the community will be for the challenges ahead. Budgeting continues to be somewhat esoteric—not many employees understand contemporary nuances of budget formation. Strategic and operational plans are different; the more employees who become good planners, the more prepared the organization will be. In my view, strategic planning is a cornerstone of public administration.

Develop Plans – Using detail and the processes described in earlier chapters, each unit that will have its own plan will then convene selected staff, meeting enough times (four to five is average) to prepare a draft plan. Plans for smaller work units average around eight pages, although some larger division plans reach fifteen or more pages. Remember that your strategic plan does not contain a lot of operational information. It deals with major strategic issues and challenges. Responsibility for plan completion exists within each organizational unit that is to have an independent plan. Department administrators and directors are responsible for ensuring divisions, bureaus, and sections have plans drafted within established time frames and are also responsible for the composite department plan that combines the essential major elements from each individual plan. The entire drafting process often takes less than four to six weeks from start to finish. After proper training and good examples, I have seen some large departments complete the process in just four weeks! That is the beauty of focusing on key issues, goals, objectives, strategies and actions and reducing narrative to virtually zero. Instead, planning is fast, targeted, and precise.

Create an Editing Team – As part of the Strategic Planning Team or as a separate group, an Editing Team is important. Again, I have learned this from hard experience. Many people are great at data collection and can generate powerful content but are not particularly adept or interested in crafting the finished document. The Editing Team is comprised of good writers who understand document preparation and receive special training to become gatekeepers for formatting, grammar, punctuation, and presentation quality. It manages the development process and ensures a quality product. It also enables work units to focus on content and leave much of the final editing/formatting to others who possess that talent. Cover development, binding, and final printing are directed by this group, which also takes each plan segment through its final stages.

Outside Review/Participation – This is always a discussion point and certainly, outside involvement can be helpful, especially to identify external issues and challenges. However, caution is urged when considering involvement in developing missions, visions, values, goals, annual objectives, and strategies. That is the role of professional administrators and managers, who *may* or may not involve outside advisors. The best bet is to hold one or more community meetings to review the plan after it is drafted, offering opportunities for community members to meet representatives of each major department. That way, people from the community can visit with department personnel on specific subject areas to offer input and advice.

Ongoing Plan Implementation/Monitoring – Once completed, plans tend to get put on the shelf. This is not because people are lazy or lack commitment. It is because the amount of work associated with daily operations in public agencies is overwhelming. Involving many employees tends to ensure that attention will be paid to identified issues and to the strategies and actions listed under performance objectives. However, structure is needed to further ensure that every program reviews its plan and uses it to guide operations. Chapter 20 reviews the variance reporting process that ensures annual review of progress toward goals.

In addition to the annual variance report, I recommend that senior administrators and managers meet with program personnel at least quarterly to review annual objectives and associated strategies/ actions. Recall that each strategy/action should have an initiation or due date. Reviewing plans to check progress demonstrates commitment to the planning process and reinforces that performance is expected. I encourage mayors, commissions, and councils to use plans as working documents to check progress and to guide policy decisions. Executive directors, senior department and division administrators should have a copy of the plan in every staff meeting and use it to review progress. At the very least, review content with managers on a monthly basis to monitor progress. Once the plan is seen as an essential management guide, it will become a standard administrative tool.

Annual Timeline – The planning process should be conducted at least annually two to four months prior to the budget process, so budgeting is performance-based and is directly linked to the plan. *Remember that plans drive budgets.* Once basic strategic planning training is complete, a format established, and an inaugural plan in place, annual updating takes about a third as much time as the initial plan. Please remember, the first year is the most difficult. After that, training and development time invested during the first year pays dividends in efficient plan updates, accurate data, clear issues, and measurable objectives. By year three, the process is part of the culture and is standard operating procedure. Employees understand and accept it, and are comfortable with performance based on standards they personally established.

Summary

Earlier, I commented that just mentioning 'strategic planning' can cause people to lament and gnash their teeth. This type of planning has been misunderstood for so long that it has developed its own culture of avoidance. That said, there is no facet of public administration more important than this element of strategic management.

Exploring the future through data analysis that provides a foundation for predictability is now more important that at any time in history. Teaching a process and imbedding it in the fabric of every public organization is essential. It requires an interest in understanding future challenges, a commitment to preparation, and a desire to build efficient, effective public agencies. The value of strategic planning lies in its process, not in its product...although having a path forward with the tangible means to both ensure and measure progress allows the best of both worlds.

It is amazing what participation can do for morale, productivity, and accountability. Keep in mind that teams are developed when they are able to identify and solve important issues; nothing builds a strong team more effectively than working together on issues important to the agency or the community.

Chapter 19

The Organization Improvement Council

Private business has invested enormous sums in lean manufacturing, Six Sigma, systems engineering, Total Quality Management, and other continuous improvement processes. As with any organization, it pays to be efficient, highly effective, and consistently productive and results oriented. Whether private or public, it is essential that a cycle of improvement be built into the organization's culture. The strategic planning process outlined in this book was developed to promote organization development and measured improvement in state and local government. By crafting objectives that contain specific measures, it is a simple matter to assess progress, whether you are reviewing internal or external issues.

Along with measuring progress toward issue-driven goals and objectives, you must also be concerned with internal issues that inhibit your ability to achieve the mission. This parallel commitment is facilitated by identifying internal issues that affect organization efficiency, effectiveness, quality, performance, and cost. Once identified, elected officials and senior administrators must address these inhibiting factors. A unique means of accomplishing this is creation of an internal Organization Improvement Council (OIC).

Purpose and Contribution

The OIC is an organizational unit that is added following strategic plan completion. Because there are typically a number of important *internal* issues identified during the planning process, common questions from employees are, *'What are we going to do about the internal issues and challenges we've identified? Will administrators or elected officials allow us to address the barriers and issues that keep us from accomplishing our mission or from being as efficient as we could be?'*

Without an organized process to follow up and monitor a variety of internal issues and challenges, they are often lost or neglected. If this occurs, employees have another reason to say, "Well, we told you that management doesn't really care about internal problems; they never intended to do anything."

Like so many organizational situations, this can lead to poor morale, resistance, reduced productivity and loss of initiative. Once expectations have been dashed, employees have a hard time rallying, especially during challenging economic times when every program is being scrutinized.

However, if internal issues and challenges are addressed through a permanent, formal Council, employees are energized because they see progress toward the identified internal issues. Once a Council is formed and begins to address inhibiting factors, I typically see more creativity, productivity, initiative, collaboration and high morale. People want progress, particularly in the internal operational world. They are paid to deal with *external* challenges in the city, county or state. But it is the *internal* issues and challenges in their workplace that marginalizes their ability to perform.

The OIC allows administrators to systematically address internal issues and challenges identified during the strategic planning process. It keeps the organization's *improvement agenda* fresh and current, while consistently reducing factors that negatively impact the five key measures: *efficiency, effectiveness, quality, productivity* and *cost*. Importantly, the Council is *neither political nor managerial*. Rather, it is comprised of employees who volunteer or are asked to work on internal issues that inhibit the organization.

Council Specifics

1. It is good to use volunteers but they must be able to bring energy, expertise and commitment to effectively address issues. Where specific talents or characteristics are needed, you may request that a particular employee serve. Council members should be from several divisions and, if the Council represents an entire city or county, have representation from all departments. Broad representation is essential.

2. The Council is *not* comprised only of managers and supervisors, although some will serve as members. Employees from various disciplines and all levels should be involved. The chair is typically a facilitator or 'convener' and is elected by OIC peers. It is best to appoint a chair at the beginning.

3. Membership is normally from five to fifteen people, depending on agency size. Some can't make every meeting, so it is fine to have a fairly large number. For a small agency, city or county, five to eight members will suffice. The key is to have engaged, interested members who can represent the agency or entire government to address internal issues.

4. The OIC is a formal but dynamic and enjoyable process, where people get along and take pride in solving internal issues. While some issues are quite serious, others are reasonably easy to solve. Take this work seriously. However, this not a place for curmudgeons, malcontents or complainers; it is a place for energetic problem-solvers who care about the agency and community and are committed to continuous improvement.

5. OIC members should be chosen by peers in their departments, *not* by senior managers. However, some managers like to have certain 'go getters' on the council to ensure a good start. Having the right membership mix is crucial.

6. As a rule, most councils meet weekly or bi-monthly, but take time to fulfill their promise. This is a new concept—that of allowing public employees to formally convene to solve internal issues,

which was formerly the sole province of management. Let the OIC work and provide ample time and operational support. A year might be needed to see good gains and fluid operation, although a lot will be done in the first few months.

7. The Council needs enough clout to make recommendations that will be valued and seriously considered. It is important that recommendations generate positive action. If resources are required to conduct analysis or gather data, provide them. The OIC is not an expensive process. Good leaders use employee councils. The only difference with an OIC is that it is tied to the strategic planning process and its charter is to address identified internal issues.

8. In a large agency, the Council organizationally sits between the director and the various divisions and bureaus. If the OIC is to serve a city or county, it sits between the various department heads and the mayor/council or commissioners and has representation from all departments. It makes recommendations to the directors, mayor and council or county commission. If it serves one department, it makes recommendations to the director and division managers. Governors may convene a special council comprised of OIC representatives from each state agency. The emphasis is to identify internal issues that are barriers to performance and efficiency then offer clear, workable solutions that will improve operations.

9. The initial OIC agenda is the entire set of internal issues and challenges identified by divisions or departments during the strategic planning process. It will combine all issues into a central listing, and then place them in categories (normally around eight to twelve.) The OIC then prioritizes the categories and the issues within each to create a working list that is driven by what is most important to the organization.

10. Priority should be determined by criteria established by senior managers and elected officials. What is important to one person might not be as important to another. The OIC needs consensus so it has a clear agenda and direction when it begins its work.

11. The most effective councils begin with the 'low hanging fruit.' That is, issues that can be easily addressed. This allows the OIC to begin with several accomplishments. This builds confidence and allows OIC members to establish a process of gathering data, conducting analysis and posing remedies that solve identified problems. So, begin with smaller issues before tackling the big ones.

12. Share information with all employees. Especially at the department level, employees have identified internal issues and will be curious if and how they are being addressed. I encourage full disclosure of the final prioritized list, all analysis and any recommended actions.

13. The OIC is *not* a policy-making body. It keeps the 'Improvement Agenda' and creates work teams termed *'Action Teams'* to address specific issues. In established OICs, there may be five to eight action teams working on issues at any given time. Once a team has a recommended solution, it is presented to the OIC for input and response. It may give guidance or may have the action team present the solution(s) to the director. If representing an entire city or county, the action team, OIC or department administrator may present to the mayor/council or county commission. However the council is positioned, appropriate decision-makers hear action team recommendations. Elected decision-makers may license department heads to go forward with solutions if funds are available or if they agree to allocate additional funding. Extensive recommendations considered valuable to the organization will always be discussed with elected officials and will often be included in subsequent budgets. The most incisive questions pertain to, *'How do we improve this organization and its ability to serve the public?'*

14. Action team membership generally comes from outside the OIC. Even though it is normal for an OIC member to sit on an action team or even to facilitate it, other members are recruited from various departments. Among action teams, the broader representation, the better. They contain subject matter experts

who address one or two issues at a time. Keep teams small and mobile with an average size of three to five people.

15. Think of the OIC as a hub of a wheel with action teams orbiting around the core council. The OIC creates action teams that work on issues until they are solved. Once an issue is resolved, its action team is disbanded or addresses a new issue. The OIC's responsibility is to ensure consistent internal improvement. It maintains an improvement agenda, conducts analysis, keeps records, and monitors Action Team progress. To be effective, an OIC must be a structural part of state and local government agencies. This is a new paradigm. It provides an open and active approach to continuous improvement, which is discussed but rarely formalized in government.

16. As with any organization of this nature, there will be setbacks but they need to be met with positive thought and action. Internally, state and local government must be more collaborative and less fearful of openly discussing internal organizational performance issues. Understand internal problems, develop an agenda, set priorities, and establish Action Teams to develop workable solutions. This will make a palpable difference in your organization's culture and will provide many positive contributions, such as:

- Increased productivity
- Higher morale
- Better decisions
- More cost-effectiveness
- Better efficiency
- More collaboration
- More cooperation
- Clearer communication
- Fewer mistakes and problems
- Higher quality
- Greater trust

Historically, senior administrators or management teams have been forced to address internal issues. For many, 20–30% of each day is dedicated to managing internal problems that could be addressed through more efficient means. For example, if several county departments identify internal issues related to motor pool use, training, archaic policies, and loss of productivity due to insufficient computing power, each issue could be addressed by an improvement council and its action teams. Gathering information, conducting analysis, drafting options, and posing recommendations can be done by Action Teams with appropriate subject matter experts. Treat each issue as a separate project with a simple project plan, timeline, and milestones.

Once the team is prepared to make its recommendation, it can do so to agency directors or appropriate elected official, providing the material necessary for an informed decision. The cardinal rule of organization development is to 'Ask the employees.' They know the issues and can usually recommend sensible solutions. Effective department directors don't abdicate problem-solving responsibilities; they collaborate to identify and implement solutions.

Establishing an OIC is a natural outcome of a collaborative planning process. It allows public employees to actively address internal issues *they* identified during the strategic planning process. This simple structure will pull people together, allow them to work on meaningful issues, and encourage cooperative solutions. It reinforces the value of annual planning and allows elected officials and administrators to see measured organizational improvement. This will have a positive impact on state and local government and on services provided to the public.

As a final note, the *legacy* you leave as participants and leaders can be profound. To achieve the greatest possible impact, an OIC must be deeply committed to problem-solving, well-informed, courageous, and interested in improving government performance. Taken together, these characteristics reflect the positive aspects of the government's culture and provide the basis for how it can continuously improve quality, service, productivity, and ultimately, value.

Chapter 20

The Annual Variance Report: Value and Approach

There is a special artistry in being able to express virtually every issue or challenge in numeric terms. Having good data helps, but there is real value in understanding that all data must pass an assessment of either being unacceptably high, too low, or within standards. As emphasized throughout this book, everything is measurable. Administrators who lament that they have insufficient data or that their work cannot be measured must recognize that data is found everywhere and that measurement is indeed possible. Maybe I am missing something, but while working with every conceivable agency of state and local government, I have never found a situation where some means of measurement could not be found.

Measurement provides the basis for quarterly and annual progress reviews. As each fiscal year ends, I recommend that all annual objectives and actions be reviewed and progress evaluated. How much progress was made? Were actions accomplished? Was there progress 'downfield' toward longer-term goals? If so, how much? Keep in mind that merely completing an activity does not mean it had value. For the time and money spent to conduct that activity or a series of activities, what desired *outcome* was achieved?

There must be a formal evaluation system that ties directly to your strategic plan. If we assume all objectives have percents or numbers, it is a simple matter to assess any change from the previous value. For example, if your objective was '*To reduce, from 27 to <22, the number of substandard bridges in the county,*' your numbers should indicate the number of newly refurbished bridges and whether you reduced the previous number of substandard bridges to a desired number. Again, data provides the baseline. You will go from a value to a value, or you will *maintain* a standard value deemed important to the community (immunization rates, EPA standards for water and air, average caseload, cost per transaction, usage levels, etc.)

Annual Variance Report Defined

The Annual Variance Report is a *progress report* based on the objectives and strategies/actions described in the strategic plan. The basis for evaluating progress is found primarily in these plan elements. Because the variance report takes its language and values directly from the strategic plan, clear linkage is maintained. Properly crafted objectives, strategies and actions provide clear, concise descriptions for each listed performance measure. Fundamentally, the report explains what actually occurred, positive or negative, for every listed objective and strategy/action. It does *not* provide detail regarding remediation strategies (corrective actions) but may provide a brief explanation as to *why expected performance was not achieved.*

Rationale

As a public administrator or elected official, I assume you would like to know what the issue was, what progress was planned, what actually occurred and why. (I always want to know what happened and why.) Did we actually reduce or increase to the desired new value? If not, why weren't we successful? If our objective was to maintain a specified standard, were we successful? If not, what happened?

> *"What gets measured gets done, what gets measured and*
> *fed back gets done well, what gets rewarded gets repeated."*
> — *John E. Jones*

Good public management requires identification of important internal and external issues, associated long-term goals, annual performance objectives for those goals, and a series of strategies and actions that indicate how each objective will be achieved. In every public plan performance measures are essential. However, another Achilles heel of public planning is the quality of implementation. Once plans are prepared, managers must establish the means of reporting and assessing progress. This makes the annual Variance Report a critical element of the planning cycle that will:

- Increase overall department and division performance

- Establish a cycle of continuous improvement

- Generate an ability to establish outputs and outcomes for objectives and actions

- Create stronger commitment to planning and measured performance

- Demonstrate value and contribution from each program unit

- Maintain connection among various issues, plan objectives, strategies, actions and outcomes

- Establish management focus on milestones and periodic performance review

Without a formal system to assess if and to what extent the measures were achieved, the planning process has no basis for analyzing contribution.

Timing

Variance reports are typically compiled annually and presented within 60–90 days of the end of the fiscal year. Ample time must be provided to compile data, review performance objectives and strategies/actions and assess what actually occurred. For larger departments, this often requires a reporting cycle that begins earlier or later. However, it is important that annual performance data is available prior to establishing next year's performance objectives. This cycle must be calibrated with annual operations planning and budget development, which is scheduled according to the fiscal year and can be a lengthy process. Less formal quarterly reviews are recommended and many organizations choose to assess monthly performance as part of normal management activities.

Good public management requires periodic reviews to assess progress and make appropriate course corrections. While most state and local governments have similarities, there are often important differences that will dictate planning and performance assessment cycles. The following general timeline may be helpful, although every state and local agency is cautioned to proceed according to existing cycles.

- Establish a timeline beginning at the end of each fiscal year. Normally, sixty days is adequate to review data and determine progress toward objectives and strategies/actions.

- Set a date when Annual Variance Reports are due.

- Set a date when all Reports will be discussed along with corrective actions.

- If there is to be a quarterly review, develop a calendar early each year and notify all managers *when* and *how* the review will take place. Encourage managers to hold informal monthly reviews.

A properly managed organization will constantly review progress toward established measures and adjust as needed to ensure progress. This develops a culture of continuous improvement wherein employees and managers consistently seek progress toward performance milestones. This also allows regular milestone review to ensure they remain viable.

Measures can be amended if circumstances change but the reason must be recorded and justified. I encourage elected officials and administrators to measure everything, review progress toward every performance indicator, and celebrate that progress. Both the community and public employees need to understand and take pride in continuous organization and community improvement. Especially in difficult times, it is essential that all elected officials, administrators and managers make every effort to become more efficient, effective and productive while operating at the lowest possible cost. America has entered a transformational era that will require extraordinary effort to balance budgets and serve growing community needs. How successful we are will depend on our collective ability to consistently meet annual objectives and inspire our colleagues to do more with less.

Key to Success

The most crucial element of the annual Variance Report is the quality of measurable objectives and the clarity of strategies/actions. If there is good numeric measurement for each objective and each strategy/action is concisely written, output and outcome measures are both easy to write and simple to assess. By now, this should be clear when reviewing the samples provided in previous chapters. As with all planning, assessment requires a baseline. If there is no baseline for the original issue and no statement of intended progress, it will be impossible to assess performance. There must be a baseline value and reasonable output or outcome measures indicating intended progress. Otherwise, there is no way to assess if progress was actually made. Adequate time and effort must therefore be applied to gathering accurate data that define issues (and their impact), developing sound objectives, and preparing concise strategies/actions. This interconnectivity becomes apparent when managers develop Variance Reports. If these elements were done well, gathering data and analyzing variance will be simple and will clearly indicate areas and means of improvement.

Constructing a Variance Report

With a plan format that has annual objectives with measurement expressed in numbers or percentages indicating an increase, reduction or status quo (maintenance), output/outcome measures are simply expressions taken from objectives, strategies and actions. Once established, these measures can be reviewed monthly or quarterly to evaluate progress. On an annual basis, each output/outcome (performance) measure is reviewed, analyzed for progress and stated in the report. For example, if the issue involved the number of cases backlogged in the police department, this would be expressed as a number that is unacceptably high and the objective would indicate that the annualized intent is '*To reduce, from* ___ *to* ___, *the number of cases currently in the system.*' Associated with this objective are strategies and a series of actions.

The Variance Report would contain the original value that was deemed too high and the *actual* reduction in case load. A simple numeric comparison reports the former value and the current value, which hopefully provides the intended reduction. If it did not produce the planned reduction, there should be an explanation of what prevented the objective from being achieved. The same is true with strategies and actions. They are listed in the Variance Report with a short description of what occurred; whether they were completed or not, to what extent they were successful, and if not, why not.

This process is similar to business management and continuous improvement systems. Objectives are established based on accepted data; strategies and action plans are developed and executed throughout the year. At the end of each quarter and annually, there is a review of what happened and why. Did we meet objectives? By how much? And, if not, why not?

I prefer simple Variance Reports that use virtually the same language found in the Strategic Plan. You have already written the goals, annual performance objectives, strategies and actions. To the extent possible the same text should be used. The following steps will help construct an annual Variance Report:

1. Copy and paste all performance objectives and their associated strategies/actions into a new document (create a new document). Follow the order exactly as the text appears in the Strategic Plan. *The exact same language should appear in the Variance Report as it appears in the Strategic Plan.* Do *not* change wording, measurement or timelines. Good plan content will provide good Variance Report content.

2. After reviewing the required data, records, etc., state what actually occurred for each objective, strategy and action. *Do not editorialize.* State what happened as precisely as possible so the

reader knows what occurred. Full sentences aren't required—
clarity is more critical.

3. Many strategies/actions are often common operational activities
    that are to be accomplished according to a specified timeline. The
    timeline becomes very important as a performance measure—
    perhaps as much as the activity. Was the action undertaken, was
    it done properly, and started/completed on time?

4. Because output/outcome measures are values expressed in
    performance objectives found in the strategic plan, they are
    already written and can be copied into the Variance Report. They
    can then be compared with actual values determined at the end of
    the annual cycle.

5. *Do not* explain here what will be done to correct performance,
    especially where performance was not achieved. That will be
    done in the next strategic plan. Focus on reporting *what* happened
    and *why*. Compare what was intended vs. what actually occurred.

6. All performance objectives and strategies/actions are addressed
    in the Variance Report.

7. *If additional actions or strategies were undertaken to accomplish a
    performance objective they may be added to the Report.* This occurs
    when managers deploy other methods or mechanisms to achieve
    an objective—ones that were not apparent during the strategic
    planning process.

8. In autonomous state and local governments, departments should
    be required to use a *single format and style* for annual variance
    reporting. Similar to a budget format, the Variance Report format
    should be created by executive management with input from
    administrators. Having a single format will preclude a hodge-
    podge of formats and styles that detract from the value of annual
    performance review.

The system developed by The Futures Corporation uses the same
strategic plan document and merely adds an area that can be expanded to

report annual outcomes and outputs based on what was stated in objectives, strategies and actions. Using the same format simplifies the annual process and drastically reduces time requirements. In my experience, one of the best systems out there is used by the Department of Public Works and Utilities in Lincoln, Nebraska. It uses its annual strategic plan as a dual-purpose planning and reporting document and has detailed numeric measures that are monitored quarterly.

Points to remember...

- Variance reports can be developed as soon as practical after the fiscal year ends, or as soon as performance data is available. Some departments may have delays in gathering data the first year, especially if there is an initial 'short' year when a new strategic planning process is also being introduced. Once the process becomes annualized, variance reporting becomes part of the yearly cycle.

- Keep the reporting format simple and amend when departments determine easier and more effective ways to report performance. Most reports are quite abbreviated, depending on the length of the strategic plan, how many objectives there are and how much detail is included.

- The Variance Report uses the list of department annual objectives with their associated strategies and actions in the same order as they appear in the strategic plan.

- Variance reports are short and concise. They provide a short assessment of current status that reviews what actually occurred relative to each objective, expressed whenever possible in numbers or percentages. Concise writing without a lot of detail or explanation is the standard. Use bullets where possible to offer a brief explanation of what occurred relative to the objective; what happened that allowed *or* precluded the organization from accomplishing the objective; what was planned and what actually occurred.

- There are always questions about the need to report on strategies and actions found under each objective. This is because it is easy for many departments to verbally review actions and strategies for each objective through informal internal meetings or in more structured meetings with a mayor, council or commission. However, it is helpful to have one written summary variance report that contains results of objectives, strategies and actions.

- The average time required for variance reporting depends on the number of annual objectives but most departments require five to ten man-days to complete reports. This can be expedited if records have been kept on performance and data has been tracked throughout the year. If done well, it takes little time to compare what was intended to what actually occurred, and why. *The first year is most difficult because there is often inadequate data on some objectives.* However, this will be naturally corrected as more performance data is tracked and recorded.

- Elected officials are typically very interested in departmental performance, so keep them in mind as you prepare your report. A governor, city manager, county administrator, mayor, council or commission will be the direct recipient of annual reports and all need assurance that departments are progressing toward annual objectives and long-term goals. Above all, they need accurate information to share with the public.

Summary

Performance planning requires measurement, analysis and reporting. Continuous improvement requires commitment to program outputs and outcomes that establish a path toward long-term goals and achieve annual performance objectives. *A variance report is simply a review of what was intended versus what was actually achieved.* Professional public administrators must be courageous enough to establish measurable performance objectives and remain committed to analyzing progress. Properly developed strategic plans contain all the elements necessary to prepare annual variance reports that indicate progress toward long-term goals.

Annual variance reports review the status of *annual* department objectives and determine if they were achieved. Generally, only the variance between what was *intended* and what was actually *achieved* is reviewed and reported. It often suffices to merely report an action as 'accomplished' to satisfy the intent of variance reporting, but the central question is whether it contributed to a desired outcome. Always remember that elected officials need accurate information to demonstrate progress and continuous improvement.

Optimally, formal variance reporting showcases a progressive posture throughout state and local government at a time when issues abound and the public is demanding measured performance, higher quality and greater value.

Chapter 21

Building a Strategic Budget

A budget is, first and foremost, a planning device that serves as a central ingredient in both strategic and general operations planning. It is also an accountability device that provides another mechanism for evaluating program performance. In many ways, when taken together, strategic and operations plans are the blueprints for change and performance; the budget is the engine that drives and energizes that change and performance.

Keep in mind that goals and objectives cost nothing; once you 'operationalize' plan elements through strategies and actions, you accrue cost. Goals and objectives indicate *what* you will accomplish; strategies and actions convey *how* you will achieve those goals and objectives. Budgets fund strategies and actions; they also fund general operations, which are the basic services provided by each government agency. Remember also that a *strategic plan* addresses *only* the major issues and challenges the organization and community is facing and *does not include general mission-driven operational actions*. Those should be included in an agency's general operations plan as part of its executive planning system.

Strategic Budgets

Properly crafted, a performance-based budget encourages improvement and annually affirms continuous improvement plans. It helps establish, legitimize, and maintain priorities while showcasing program intent and important contributions.

A strategic budget links to the issues/challenges, annual objectives, strategies and actions identified in the strategic plan. It must integrate an annual review of program outputs and outcomes and always focus on the organization's strategic direction and intent. Clear, hard quantification and measurement must be part of an annual budget review, but evaluative data should come directly from the programs. This encourages all bureaus, divisions, and departments (and government generally) to maintain good numeric records and to carefully record both outputs and outcomes. It also encourages them to relate how those outputs and outcomes influence identified issues and challenges. If a legislature, city council, city manager, school board, utility district, board of aldermen, county administrator or county commission expects program improvement, the budget is the perfect place to annually showcase it.

A strategic budget...

- Focuses on improvement
- Deals with program specifics
- Relates to the program mission
- Is driven by program issues
- Funds strategies and actions
- Uses quantification from strategic plans
- Allocates funds to strategic issues and seeks a significant return for the dollars spent

When reviewing this list, keep in mind that we are discussing a *strategic* budget. An *operational* (or operations) budget is that facet of the budget that contains funding for basic operations and whatever expansion or contraction is planned for the coming year. Therefore, a comprehensive budget has two aspects; it is both *strategic* and *operational*. As a strategic thinker, you are focusing on critical strategic issues that either are known (such as the number of substandard bridges, traffic congestion, crime rates, etc.), or have the potential to become events or create situations that could have catastrophic (or at least serious) consequences for constituents or the entire community. As an elected official, administrator, or program manager, you must successfully operate in two related worlds—strategic *and* operational. And, those worlds constantly fluctuate as integrated dimensions of public management.

The Challenge of Budget – Plan Linkage

Over the four decades I have studied public sector strategic planning, there have been many discussions with elected officials and professional administrators about linking budgets to plans. To understate the challenges would be a disservice to the many dedicated public administrators and managers who have shared their frustrations about having critical issues ignored by elected decision-makers during budget planning. Because I have also experienced this frustration as a program manager in both state and local government, it is probably worth discussing some of the inhibiting factors.

The most commonly voiced concern by experienced public managers, especially at the program level, is that, while they are subject matter experts who might identify a serious issue and recommend appropriate strategies to address that issue, elected officials may argue, ignore, or otherwise counter a specific funding request. Quite often, this neglect compounds the identified issue and adds costs as the situation deteriorates to crisis levels.

To be fair, elected officials are in a terribly difficult position. There are often insufficient funds to support even basic services and deferred maintenance has created across America a crisis of epic proportions. Roads, bridges, levees, dams, schools, airports, ports, water and wastewater systems, crime, immunization levels, security systems, and basic administrative systems are inadequate throughout state and local government. Facilities and equipment are often insufficient to accomplish required tasks and programs cannot meet public expectations.

Elected officials must contend with powerful conflicting interests while resorting to serial triage to maximize available tax dollars, often neglecting one program to support another. And, it will get worse as the U.S. continues to transform into a more integrated global economic power with fewer independent resources, more international competition and less clout than in previous decades.

Deferred maintenance will forever be seen as a major contributor to current problems. According to a 2009 EPA report, at least $335 billion will be required just to maintain the nation's drinking water system in the coming decades. The EPA estimates that annual budgeting for water systems is $22 billion short of what is required. Similar issues exist with roads, levees, dams, wastewater systems, ports, airports, and many other essential public facilities. There are trillions of dollars needed to address critical strategic public issues that are growing more severe.

For state, city and county administrators, along with department and division managers, the challenge is to share hard data that tells the appropriate story. When coaching administrators, I encourage them to provide clear data that showcases the magnitude of strategic issues and demonstrates their potential impact if not addressed. Once elected decision makers understand the issue and its ramifications, the burden is on them to make the best possible informed decision. As emphasized earlier, it won't get any easier in the next decade.

There are several factors that inhibit proper linkage between strategic plans and budgets. Among the most significant are:

- The disparity in budgeting philosophy and planning styles.

- Adversarial history between program managers and elected officials.

- Feelings of agency vulnerability- fear of losing funding or power.

- Lack of historic cooperative planning throughout state and local government.

- Most strategic plans are poorly crafted and have little real measurability.

- Confusion about operations budgets vs. strategic budgets.

- Focus has not been on measured improvement.

- Zero-basing is confused with performance-basing.

- Insufficient training in public sector strategic planning and performance-based budgeting – and how to forge an integrated performance budget from operations, strategic and improvement plans.

Key Elements of Budget Linkage

Fortunately, most public agencies already have sound budget processes, so there is really no need to re-engineer what already works. As I visit with various state and local governments, it appears that far too many agencies re-engineer to find magic when recalibration and training is all that is needed. Content is the critical factor. Budgets are mostly process and timing; many administrators forget that quality content and metrics make great performance-based budgets. Some also call these 'outcome-based' budgets but they all seek the ability to reflect progress toward goals.

To develop strong performance-based budgets that tie directly to your strategic plan, the following guidelines are recommended:

- If you have a good budget process, continue to use the same system with appropriate refinements and training in strategic plan linkage.

- Each program unit must have a strategic plan or the process is weakened.

- Remember that the strategic performance-based budget element is *in addition to* the bulk of the budget that deals with basic operations. The majority of all budgeting relates to maintenance of basic operations. If you have an operations plan (or at least an existing outcome-based budget), it will contain performance indicators that provide the basis for measurement. Budgets should have performance measures from both *strategic* and *operations* plans.

- From the strategic plan, use measures found in annual performance objectives and various actions that indicate outputs or outcomes.

- Throughout the entire organization, performance reporting ties directly to objectives and strategies/actions from each program's strategic plan. As noted, the budget will also contain performance metrics from each operating element of every department.

- Don't try to put *everything* in the budget. Focus on the major issues found in the strategic plan and performance measures listed in the operations plan, indicating how you will measure operational performance. Large departments may have to winnow issues and submit budget requests for only a portion of those issues identified by division, bureau and section managers. There will never be enough money to address every identified issue. However, annually 'showcasing' key issues keeps them on the radar screen while emphasizing their relevance and potential to harm constituents or the general community.

- Annually, as new issues are identified or continued from previous years, administrators will find that some high priority issues and their associated objectives, strategies and actions can be addressed with available funding. By shifting internal priorities, those issues can still be addressed without new funds.

- Relative to the strategic plan, focus on outputs and outcomes that make a significant impact on existing community issues, program objectives and goals; deal with planned achievement and allocate financial resources accordingly.

As an elected official or administrator, you must operate in two worlds— strategic and operational. And, those worlds constantly fluctuate as integrated dimensions of public management.

- Always remember that budgets are based on plans—not the other way around—plan first, then develop the budget to gain the greatest value. *Plans drive budgets.*

The real value of linking budgets with program planning is that decision-makers begin to appreciate issues showcased in each department strategic plan and calculate how financial resources might facilitate improvement. Resources are limited, so every allocated dollar must pay a dividend. Creating performance budgets linked to strategic plans will ensure that issues important to the community are annually addressed and that limited funds have the greatest positive impact.

Budgeting will become even more controversial as tax dollars remain generally constant as service demands grow and public expectations escalate. Executive management must embrace three dimensions of public administration—strategic planning, operational planning and internal improvement planning. Historically, training in public administration has not addressed these three areas very effectively. Many managers are unaware of how various planning tools can be effectively linked to performance-based budgets to demonstrate progress toward operational and strategic goals. Training at all levels is essential.

However, two to three days of training is typically all that is needed to understand performance measures, identify key strategic and operational measures from each department and link to a strategic budget. Once this level of understanding is achieved, it creates a platform that allows plans to drive budgets while establishing annual budgets as fully integrated, pivotal performance management tools.

While many citizens have the erroneous perception that government offices are flush with ample money, space, staff, training and equipment, the opposite is actually true. For the output expected, many state and local government agencies have too few people, inadequate or insufficient equipment, marginal facilities, and funding that is insufficient to accomplish various missions. Certainly, many state and local government agencies are amply staffed and equipped, but without sustained funding levels that accompany population growth, they, too, will see steady decline.

Chapter 22

A Time of Transformation, Courage and Leadership

As you contemplate the path forward, I encourage you to consider several things. First, change will occur no matter what you do. It is part of social, biological, economic and geologic evolution. Regardless of your views concerning constituent or community preparation and foresight, time refuses to stop. Rather, it seems to be accelerating at a pace that compresses global progress into uncountable sound bites and an information deluge. Keep in mind that the future is what matters. While history is important and is a retrospective window into a relevant past, it cannot map the future. I am amused at the constant rhetoric about change when the real discussion should be about preparing for a very challenging future. My message: Get ready…*NOW*.

Realize that the concept of strategic thought pertains to how you contemplate the future and the challenges it brings to your state, community and, of course, this nation. Focus on questions that are relevant to those you represent: the citizen stakeholders who expect so much at a time when there is less to give. As stated throughout this book, you are all futurists; you are strategic thinkers who are at the helm during a transformational time in this nation's history. More accurately, you and your colleagues across many nations are on watch during one of the most significant transformational eras in world history. If you don't believe that, you're just not paying attention.

Strategic thinkers are adaptive to changing events and circumstances. They are 'prepared for challenge,' which has been the 'flagship' program of The Futures Corporation for over twenty-five years. We believe in the future, so constantly ask community leaders, '*Are you prepared?*'

There are several characteristics of strategic thinkers that I would encourage you to build into your personal and professional development. From what I have seen and experienced, strategic thinkers:

- Have a can-do attitude that allows them to be leaders during difficult times.

- Love data and use it to build platforms that both ensure and measure performance.

- Try new things because they are unafraid to innovate and support the creativity of others.

- Remain confident, open and collaborative in the face of difficult new challenges.

- Are expert learners who constantly and willingly share information.

- Are customer/community centered, i.e. are 'servant leaders.'

- Seek to truly understand issues before posing solutions.

- Understand that public sector strategic plans are uniquely issue-driven and essential for developing vibrant, progressive communities.

Over many years, I have been amazed by the resilience, spirit and competence of public employees. Those who denigrate public servants are normally those who have never served in city, county, state or federal government. In this new and uncertain age, we need to attract talent with new ideas and the courage to confront new realities. And, we need to celebrate and support current employees who labor every day in an environment growing more unstable due to the enormous nationwide conflict between debt and demand.

A Time for Renewal

As we approach 2011, the 2010 federal budget deficit is projected to exceed $1.3 trillion, with a cumulative national debt burden close to or exceeding $13 trillion. The 2009 deficit of $1.4 trillion equaled almost 10% of the nation's GDP. In 2001, the U.S. had an annual budget surplus of $236 billion. President Bush enacted tax cuts that transformed the surplus into a $150 billion deficit within one year—a net turnaround of $386 billion. Costs associated with 9/11 response, including wars in both Afghanistan and Iraq, added another $1 trillion in unbudgeted liabilities, and are still climbing. According to the Congressional Budget Office, the Medicare drug benefit enacted in 2003 will add another $1 trillion to the deficit by 2015. More recently, greater damage was caused by the 2007–2008 Great Recession, which saw tax receipts fall by 17%. This was in parallel to TARP funds being allocated to rescue failing businesses, considered by most economists as essential to avoid economic disaster. This is classic cost escalation with revenue decline, creating a growing chasm between available funds and operating needs.

About 55% of the federal budget consists of entitlements such as Medicare and Social Security, and billions are spent on farm subsidies and military expenditures that seem to be sacred cows. Not to mention federal and many state government pension funds that are drastically underfunded. Something has to give, even if it is a general, across-the-board percentage reduction of all programs and funds. But that takes bipartisan political will, foresight and a commitment to *confront reality.* Will that happen before more serious issues arise?

As worrisome as all these issues are, they do not consider general state and municipal debt. While state and local government is prohibited from deficit spending, the collective debt load has skyrocketed. State and local debt was stable during the 1990s, but had soared from $1.19 trillion in 2000 to $1.85 trillion by 2005—a 55% increase. Of this, approximately 39% of the total is state debt and 61% is local debt. As most readers understand, state and local debt generally takes the form of long-term municipal bonds, so citizens do not often feel the pain of such debt if there are no tax increases. Yet, government entities continue to go further into debt or reduce programs, which can pose serious problems if a catastrophic event, such as hurricane or earthquake, occurs.

Water and wastewater systems, ports, levees, roads, airports, bridges, schools, and other basic infrastructure requirements that have been deferred will add trillions of dollars to federal, state and local debt. Yet, if deference continues, more catastrophic failures will surely occur with even more disastrous financial consequences. There is little doubt that we are living on a very thin edge with high debt, declining infrastructure, growing demand, and reduced revenue potential.

The real conundrum is how to generate confidence, recover trust, reduce expenditures and boost economic vitality in the current environment. As I have often noted in my Public Futures Blog, when asked whether they favor higher program spending, lower taxes, or a balanced budget, Americans answer, 'Yes!'

What role do public administrators, division managers, and section chiefs have in the current situation? Public administrators cannot control public sentiment nor can they alter historic circumstances that created current reality. What public leaders *can* do is understand that public agencies are the centerpiece of every community. They are the foundation for safety, security, health, mobility, and quality of life. In an ambiguous and difficult world, people are seeking stability. State and local government provides that fundamental aspect of American society.

As you go forward in this current climate as strategic thinkers and planners, I encourage you to do several things:

- Separate the essential from the expendable. Determine what is required to sustain a quality community and to prepare it for the future.

- Set boundaries guided by the essential. Confront the realities of triage and what probabilities might impact the community.

- Provide rationale for what is truly important. Data expresses reality better than rhetoric. Never forget that people gravitate to leaders who provide clarity, direction, and truth in a harmonious style.

- Always maintain a community focus; challenges and solutions must be inclusive.

- Preserve a core foundation for community stability and growth. Whatever challenges arise, maintain the central cornerstones of your community, as defined by the community.

- Maintain short-term operational and longer-term strategic plans; one without the other, or a convoluted planning approach, weakens your ability to chart a meaningful course.

- Design a culture that encourages strategic thinking and innovation. Government at all levels must seek new systems, new paradigms, and a culture that promotes foresight about, and preparation for, a challenging future.

Strategic thinkers do not try to control the pace of change, nor do they fail to abandon the expendable. You cannot keep every program forever. Adapt. Grow. Address new challenges. Strategic thinkers don't express fear of the future; they study the data, interpret its meaning and pose solutions that avoid, correct, moderate or prevent. Leaders do not detach from their jobs and assume a bunker mentality, avoiding new challenges and assignments. They engage with renewed passion and commitment to the community.

Granted, it is impossible to eliminate uncertainty. It is considered one of the principal characteristics of the emerging future. Yet, there is much you can predict and prepare for. You are the keepers of the special *legacy* that is public leadership. As I see it, community leaders, elected officials, public administrators and managers at all levels of state and local government are the essential keys to a 21st Century transformation. You are pathfinders who will chart a course to a strategic future. It will be a remarkable journey.

Bibliography

Bloom, C., *Strategic Planning in the Public Sector*. (Journal of Planning Literature, 1986, 1 (2), 253-259)

Bradford, Robert W. and Duncan, Peter, *Simplified Strategic Planning – A No-Nonsense Guide for Busy People who Want Results Fast!* (Worcester, MA Chandler House Press, 2000)

Brown, Lester R., *Plan B 2.0: Rescuing a Planet Under Stress and a Civilization in Trouble*, Earth Policy Institute, (New York, NY W.W. Norton and Company, 2006)

Brown, Lester R., *Plan B 4.0: Mobilizing to Save Civilization*, Earth Policy Institute, (New York, NY, W.W. Norton and Company, 2009)

Bruce, Andy and Langdon, Ken, *Strategic Thinking*, (New York, NY, Dorling Kinderly Publishing, 2000)

Bryson, John M., *Strategic Planning for Public and Nonprofit Organizations: A Guide to Strengthening and Sustaining Organizational Achievement*, (San Francisco, CA, Jossey-Bass Publishers, 1988)

Byars, Lloyd L., *Strategic Management: Formulation and Implementation, Concepts and Cases*, Third Edition (New York, NY, HarperCollins, 1991)

Dalton, Linda C., Hoch, Charles, J., and So, Frank S., eds. *The Practice of Local Government Planning,* (Washington D.C., International City/ County Management Association Press, Third Edition, 2000)

Deming, D. Edwards, *Out of the Crises*, (Boston, MA, MIT Press, 1986)

Deming, D. Edwards, *The New Economics for Industry, Government, Education*, 2nd Edition, (Boston, MA, MIT Press, 2000)

Fogg, C. Davis, *Team-Based Strategic Planning: A Complete Guide to Structuring, Facilitating, and Implementing the Process*, (New York, NY, AMACOM Publishing, 1994)

Goodstein, Leonard D., Goodstein, Jeanette, and Nolan, Timothy, *Applied Strategic Planning: An Introduction*, (San Francisco, CA, Pfeiffer, 2008)

Haines, Stephen, *The Systems Thinking Approach to Strategic Planning and Management*
(Boca Raton, FL, CRC Press LLC, 2000)

Hendry, John and Johnson, Gerry, eds. *Strategic Thinking Leadership and the Management of Change*, (London UK, John Wiley and Sons, 1994)

Horne, Terry, and Wootton, Simon, *Strategic Thinking: A Step-by-Step Approach to Strategy*, (London, NJ, Kogan Page, Ltd. 1997, 2001)

Juran, Joseph M., *Juran on Planning for Quality*, (New York, NY, The Free Press, 1988)

Juran, Jospeh M., *Managerial Breakthrough, The Classic Book on Improving Management Performance*, (New York, NY, McGraw-Hill, 1995)

Kaufman, Roger, *Mapping Educational Success: Strategic Thinking and Planning for School Administrators*, (Thousand Oaks, CA, Corwin Press, Inc., 1995)

Luthy, John F., *Strategic Planning: A Guide for Public Managers,* International City/ County Management Association Press, IQ Report Vol. 34/No. 8, 2002

Luthy, John F., *Operations Planning for Improved Performance in a Tough Economy*, International City/ County Management Association Press, IQ Report Vol. 4/1No. 6, 2009

Mintzberg, Henry, *The Rise and Fall of Strategic Planning*, (New York, NY, Macmillan, Inc., 1994)

Morrisey, George L., *Management by Objectives and Results in the Public Sector*, (Reading, MA, Addison-Wesley Publishing, 1976)

Morrissey, George L., *Morrissey on Planning: A Guide to Strategic Thinking, Building Your Planning Foundation*, (San Francisco, CA, Jossey-Bass, 1996)

Robert, Michel, *The New Strategic Thinking Pure and Simple*, (New York, NY, McGraw-Hill, 2006)

Sanders, T. Irene, *Strategic Thinking and the New Science-Planning in the Midst of Chaos, Complexity and Change* (New York, NY, The Free Press, 1998)

Sloan, Julia, *Learning to Think Strategically*, (Burlington, MA, Butterworth-Heinemann, 2006)

Taleb, Nassim, *The Black Swan: The Impact of the Highly Improbable*, (New York, NY, Random House, 2007)

van der Heijden, Kees, *Scenarios, The Art of Strategic Conversations*, (Hoboken, NJ, John Wiley and Sons, 2005)

Weick, K., *The Social Psychology of Organizing*, (Reading, MA, Addison-Wesley, 1979)

Wells, Stuart, *Choosing the Future: The Power of Strategic Thinking*, (Boston, MA, Butterworth-Heinemann, 1998)

About the Author

John Luthy is a nationally known public sector futurist who has enjoyed a distinguished thirty-five year career serving in both government and industry. He holds a bachelor's degree in biology, a master's degree in public health, a master's degree in public administration/political science, and a doctorate in education. During his years in government, he served in local and state government in director or senior management positions in general administration, health, and human services.

Over the three decades he has consulted to private business, voluntary, and public agencies, John has assisted hundreds of organizations, including Fortune 500 corporations, closely held businesses, non-profit organizations, and city, county and state government toward the goal of becoming more productive, cohesive, and accountable. He is the creator of the acclaimed *Prepared For Challenge™ Organization Development Series*, which has guided hundreds of organizations to higher levels of efficiency and performance. His feature articles, *Leaving a Leadership Legacy* and *Seven Dimensions of Employee Improvement and Development* for *Public*

Management Magazine, and *The Strategic Planning Guide* and *Operations Planning for Improved Performance in a Tough Economy* for the International City/County Management Association have received national attention. He has provided unique planning work for many communities and public agencies and his innovative strategic thinking and scenario planning processes are being used throughout the United States. Dr. Luthy is the creator of the ***Public Futures Blog*** (www.publicfuturesblog.com), which helps state and local government prepare for a challenging future, is an active member of the World Future Society and has been recognized in *'Who's Who In America'* and *'Who's Who in American Education.'* He serves as faculty for the Northwest Community Development Institute and is one of this country's most sought after keynote speakers and consultants in the areas of public sector strategic thinking, scenario planning, and preparing communities and organizations for a challenging future.

Are you

Prepared For Challenge™*?*

Watch for more books in the

Prepared For Challenge™

Public Leadership Series

From

Borderline
Publishing

Stay current! Subscribe to

www.publicfuturesblog.com

See Public Futures at www.futurescorp.com